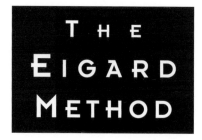

THE
EIGARD
METHOD

Eigard,Lea.
    Lifetime facial fitness without plastic surgery : the
Eigard method/Lea Eigard   1st ed.
    p. cm.
    Includes index.
    LCCN 2002114607
    ISBN 0-9725449-2-5

    1. Facial exercises. 2. Beauty, Personal.
I. Title. II. Title: Eigard method

    RA778.E345 2003   646.726
                 QB102-201042

Readers and users of the information contained in this book are strongly cautioned to consult with a physician or other health care professional before beginning any diet or fitness program.

The authors, the publishers, and any other parties make no representations or guarantees that any of the information contained in this book will produce any particular medical or physical result and none of said parties is engaged in the business of offering medical advice as a result of writing or publishing this book or otherwise making the information available. The information in this book is provided on an "AS IS" basis without any warranties of any kind, express or implied. The author, the publisher, and any other party expressly disclaim any liability for any loss or damage. We have used many sources, including our own professional and personal experience, to compile the information included in this book. This book is based on information believed to be accurate and reliable. Every effort has been made to make the book complete and accurate, but such completeness and accuracy is not guaranteed.

Warnings

For anyone with temporomandibular joint (TMJ) syndrome, back problems, or any neck or jaw injury: Do not extend your jaw or apply any pressure to your jaw when you perform the exercises. If you have any kind of back problem, sitting or lying down while you exercise will give you maximum support.

A note for readers with corrected vision: If you wear glasses, please remove them prior to beginning an exercise session. You may have to put them on in order to read the instructions and then take them off again. Contact lens wearers take special note: It is essential that you remove your lenses before performing the eye and forehead area exercises. If you can't take them out at the time, don't do the eye exercises!

And lastly, a special note for readers with long fingernails: You may find the hand positions for some of these exercises difficult if your nails are extremely long. Use extreme caution, particularly around the eyes. You should not attempt exercise No. 8 (advanced) or No. 9 (beginning and advanced) if your nails are very long and sharp.

As with any new exercise program, be sure to check with your medical doctor before starting the program described in The Eigard Method.

Printed in China

Book design by Debra Valencia, DeVa Communications
Edited by PeopleSpeak
Photos by Dina S. Khouri
Cover design by Debra Cohen
Cover photos by Pam Young
Photo editing and image enhancement by Nick Tabri, GT–XL
Photo color correction by Jon Connan, it STUDIOS
Illustrations by John Fox
Exercise Consultant, Tara Sizlo, A.C.S.M.
Indexing by J. Naomi Linzer

The Eigard Method

Lifetime Facial Fitness

without Plastic Surgery

Lea Eigard

TOLA PUBLISHING

Beverly Hills, California

About the Author

At fifty-five years of age, Lea Eigard is widely regarded
as a leading paramedical aesthetician. She is also a
licensed cosmetologist, a certified massage therapist,
and a former professional ballerina. Having combined
her knowledge of health, nutrition, and human
physiology, she has put together the most
comprehensive facial fitness program ever imagined.
Eigard has enlightened thousands about surgery-free
ageless beauty. She conducts speaking engagements for
Epicuren and offers training to those interested in
becoming instructors of The Eigard Method. Her
reputation has garnered Eigard much media attention
over the years; featured on television, on radio, and in
print, her innovative brand of facial rejuvenation has
made Lea Eigard as well known as some of
the very high profile celebrity clientele who
frequent her Beverly Hills salon.

It is with deep, heartfelt affection that I
dedicate this book

to my beautiful grandchildren,
Samantha Anne and Devin Eigard.

❧

Acknowledgments

My dear friends in the Lord, to whom I owe so much for the unwavering belief
when this project was only a dream.

Beverly Cook   Mylene Patterson   Karen Plessala   Helinda Salonga
Karen Sanchez   Holly Siniscal   Sandy Turner

To Debra Cohen for all of her hard work and dedication
in giving form to my dream.

To Debra Valencia, thank you ever so much for coloring in my dream.

To contributing writer Hillary Johnson for her revisions and adaptations.

To Stephanie Guerra, whose fingerprints are all over this book;
thank you so much for your tireless dedication.

Thanks to Nick Tabri for his work with the preface.

I am so grateful for the warmth and continuous prayers of the
Sunday school ministry and Bible study group.

For the unconditional love of my family; the rock upon which I stand, and
for my son, Eric, whose strength has comforted me so.

SOLI DEO GLORIA

Table of Contents

Table of Contents

Foreword

To feel beautiful, you must first feel comfortable—comfortable not just with your outward appearance but most especially with the process by which you achieve your outward appearance. In my twenty years spent in private practice as an aesthetic, restorative, cosmetic dermatologist, I have seen patients suffer severe anxiety and even trauma caused by both the contemplation and completion of "plastic surgery."

Fortunately, you have options. Startling and lasting results can be attained through a combination of alternative treatments, none of which are as invasive or potentially injurious as surgery. By taking a synergistic approach to facial restoration, you can keep your face and neck healthy and youthful well into your autumn years without ever experiencing the fear and discomfort that invariably accompany cosmetic surgery.

Facial exercises that strengthen and tighten the understructure of the face and neck, as well as the use of topical products coupled with noninvasive phototherapy/ laser treatment to stimulate elastic tissue and collagen, are truly the new wave in facial restoration. The key really is laying the foundation of strong and healthy muscles beneath the skin. All of these methods, properly utilized, will give the face, neck, and chest skin a fresher, firmer, and more youthful look well beyond the scope of the synthetic "surgical look" and without the unnecessary risk.

I have worked with Lea Eigard for the last five years and have the utmost respect for the principles set forth in The Eigard Method. She has incorporated into her technique the doctrines of medicine, fitness, and nutrition, and she has put together the most methodical and meticulous regimen for facial fitness imaginable. Read, learn, and enjoy the process of natural restoration.

—Harold A. Lancer, M.D., F.A.A.D.,
Assistant Clinical Professor of Dermatology,
UCLA School of Medicine

Preface

With the possible exception of Oscar Wilde's *The Picture of Dorian Gray*, this book is the single most effective guide to surgery-free ageless beauty ever written. I regard this statement as true because I have spent a lifetime making it so.

Some of my earliest memories are of my parents' beauty salon in Northern California; I blinked, it seems, and I awoke as the preteen my father would bring in to answer phones and serve coffee to their preening clientele. I blinked again and was left wishing that I had kept my eyes open just a little bit wider and maybe a little more often. It was 1969 when my father and I laid my mother, a victim of cancer, to rest. She was only forty-nine years old and I hadn't seen enough of her.

A trained ballerina, I spent most of my teenage years dancing with the Pacific Ballet in San Francisco, but it gave me great comfort to join my father at work in his salon after my mother's untimely death. It was an honor to pick up where she had left off. Helping people to look beautiful and feel good and, of course, being with my father, filled me with great joy.

Time passed, the hurt went away, and just as I could feel the gap in my heart left by my mother's passing beginning to close, tragedy struck again when my father fell ill with cancer in 1975. To combat the disease, he adopted what is often called a Paleolithic diet, consisting of mostly meat, fruits, and vegetables—with no grains and no milk or milk products. The diet sent his cancer—so often a ruthless disease resistant to modern medicine's most sophisticated drugs—into remission and ultimately extended his life by more than five years. Watching my father overcome such terrible odds simply by taking care of his body was a revelation. I was spellbound by the transformative power of diet and exercise, which in turn prompted me to learn everything I could about health, nutrition, and human physiology. In the meantime, my dad's treatment was so successful, his doctors told him that he would outlive his cancer, but his old habits proved too hard to break. He resumed his poor eating habits and in 1982, within nine months of abandoning his dietary regimen, cancer claimed his life.

I was devastated.

And then my face, like Dorian's portrait, began to wear the scars that were weathering my soul. I was aging prematurely; the stress, the sleepless nights, the grueling days, they were all piling on top of each other on top of me. Soon after, although I was still numb from the loss of my father, I nonetheless felt every blow delivered by the brutal divorce proceedings that left me in debt and outdoors. If not for the generosity of friends kind enough to provide me a place to lay my head, I would never have landed on my feet. My journey took me to Los Angeles where I began working beside some of the very best dermatologists in the business.

Beverly Hills is, and was at the time of my divorce, perhaps the largest concentric circle of stretched, stitched, and sutured faces in the world. As a paramedical aesthetician, I had seen enough badly botched face-lifts to know that cosmetic surgery was not for me. This is when I really began to develop what was to become The Eigard Method: the carefully designed facial fitness program through which the muscles of the face can be re-educated and restructured. *Without* surgery.

Do you exercise your body to look better? Or maybe just to maintain your physique? Chances are, you do. But do you exercise your face? Well, you should. Whether you want to look better or simply maintain your youthful appearance, it is absolutely imperative that you condition your facial musculature. The basic tenets of a bodily workout are my guiding principles: work out your face, just as you would work out your body—with a series of controlled movements engineered to isolate and reshape an individual muscle or muscle group.

Cultivating this idea, researching it, practicing and documenting the exercises—all of these things helped me through the most difficult time in my life. But The Eigard Method did so much more than just restore my youthful appearance. By pouring myself into its development after experiencing so much emotional pain, well, it felt good to feel good, to be excited about something. Indeed, the inspiration for The Eigard Method certainly seemed divine considering my parents' dedication to the beauty industry. How poetic then, that, after so many years as a professional ballerina, after countless hours spent training the muscles of my body in pursuit of Art, I would find myself teaching people how to train their facial muscles, like my parents, in pursuit of Beauty.

So I traded my leotards for lab coats, exchanged one branch of Aesthetics for another, and have dedicated the last fifteen years of my life to developing my theory into a discipline, very often exploring the benefits of the program with the many high-profile, celebrity clientele who frequent my Beverly Hills salon. Mine is not the only life that has been changed by The Eigard Method. I am so excited about this book and you should be too, because it really is a surgery-free guide to a firmer face. You hold in your hands a healthy and safe way to achieve truly ageless beauty. Whether you are an individual learning the exercises for yourself, or a student training to become an instructor of The Eigard Method, I bid you congratulations on your discovery and wishing you the best on your journey.

How to Use This Book

The Eigard Method can be as easy or as challenging as you want it to be. You can devote twenty minutes a day to the full program, incorporating a relaxing Warm Up and Cool Down exercise massage, or you can perform one tension-relieving exercise at a time, whenever you have a few moments to yourself.

This book is designed to be a tool you can refer to as you progress. Each exercise in the beginning series is intensified in the advanced section. Ideally, you should master the beginning version of each exercise before moving on. In some exercise books, the beginning exercises are insultingly simple, but you will not find that to be the case here.

After carefully reading the introductory material, beginners may want to spend the first couple of sessions practicing the two basic set positions in front of a mirror, alternating the "hard face" with the "soft face" (pages 12–15). If you do them correctly, your facial muscles will be sore for a couple of days just from practicing these two positions.

Alternatively, you could start by practicing just three of the ten beginning exercises. You can choose any three, but try to select one from each of the major muscle areas: neck and jaw, cheeks and lips, and eyes and forehead. Pick the exercises that speak to you and master them. Individuals learn at different paces so feel free to design your own program.

Once you've worked your way through the set positions and beginning exercises, you should be ready to tackle the advanced level. Here you may want to add one new exercise at a time to your daily workout. This doesn't mean you're a slow learner. In all my years of teaching The Eigard Method, I've yet to encounter a student who could learn all the exercises in a single session. In fact, some quite intelligent students require several sessions just to master a single advanced exercise. Just remember, if the advanced version of an exercise is easy you probably aren't doing it correctly.

Beauty of whatever kind, in its supreme development, invariably excites the sensitive soul to tears.

—Edgar Allen Poe

Introduction

Introduction

The Eigard Method is a complete facial fitness program designed to give you the same benefits as a face-lift without surgery. It is a system of precise, controlled exercises designed to prevent or reverse signs of aging in the face. In particular, the individual exercises are targeted at tightening up the neck and jawline, plumping up the cheeks and lips, and smoothing out the eye and forehead areas. The method works by strengthening and rebuilding the face's underlying muscle tissue, giving your skin the support it needs to look youthful. And unlike a surgical face-lift, the effects of which last a mere ten to fifteen years, the results achieved with The Eigard Method can last a lifetime.

If you are feeling too impatient to wait for results, think of it this way: in the time it takes to recover from an invasive surgical procedure, you could be seeing real improvement with The Eigard Method. By spending a few minutes each day practicing this step-by-step exercise program, which emphasizes correct facial posture while building strength through resistance training, you can give yourself a face-lift that won't leave you looking like a test pilot in a wind tunnel. Better yet, if you're still young and firm, you can have fuller lips and higher cheekbones than those you were born with by practicing The Eigard Method.

Your Questions Answered

Below are answers to some of the most common questions new students have regarding The Eigard Method:

How does it work?

The Eigard Method is a strength-training program based on isometric and isotonic muscle contractions. Let's take a moment to explain the difference between the two:

An *isometric* exercise is one in which the muscle simply tenses, straining against an immovable object without lengthening or shortening. Pushing against a wall or squeezing a ball are very basic and familiar examples of isometric exercise. In The Eigard Method, we sometimes use the fingers to provide tiny, controlled points of resistance, working the facial muscles against them.

An *isotonic* exercise is one in which the muscle "works" by lengthening and shortening as it moves through a range of motion while under load. This load is called resistance. A simple biceps curl is a good example of an isotonic exercise: the biceps muscle lengthens as the arm is extended and shortens during the curl. The barbell provides the resistance. In the exercises you will learn in The Eigard Method, resistance is provided solely by the hands and fingers. A few of the exercises don't introduce any external resistance at all until you have reached the advanced level.

For you Latin lovers, "isometric" comes from *iso,* meaning same, and *metric,* meaning length. "Isotonic" comes from *iso* meaning same, and *tonic,* meaning tension.

What is facial posture?

Remember all those times your mother told you not to make that silly expression or your face would "get stuck that way"? It turns out that she was right. She probably also told you to sit up straight in your chair and to square your shoulders when you walk. If you listened to her and developed good posture habits, you probably don't suffer endlessly from backaches or neck pain. The Eigard Method is designed to teach you the correct habits of facial posture that your mother instinctively knew existed.

It's true, the face has posture—good or bad—just like the body. In the course of day-to-day living, most of us develop poor facial posture. We sleep with our faces mashed into a pillow, we purse our lips when concentrating, we scowl when tense, we squint when driving into the sun, or we develop a permanent smoker's pucker. The best route to physical grace and poise is the study of martial arts or classical ballet, and The Eigard Method is the only exercise system designed to accomplish the same results for the face.

Good facial posture brings with it a long list of lasting benefits. Most students come in search of beauty, but many have happily reported headache and neck pain relief from practicing The Eigard Method.

Do I have to do all ten of the exercises every day?

Each of the ten exercises in The Eigard Method works a majority of the fifty-seven muscles of the face and neck. This means that any program you can stick to will be a balanced one. Even if you choose to start with a single exercise performed once a day, you will be getting a complete workout, building muscle strength and toning the face. This is because The Eigard Method is not based on repetition but rather on precise, concentrated, and methodical execution.

How long will it take me to learn the exercises?

Those who have studied fitness systems for the body (students of dance, yoga, ballet, weightlifting, Pilates, and so on) may learn more quickly than others, but even fitness fanatics will find these exercises challenging. Unlike other facial exercise systems, which teach you to work one muscle at a time, The Eigard Method is a complex discipline and requires practice and effort. Of course, this is also why it works so well. The good news is that you will see positive results from The Eigard Method long before you achieve mastery.

How long will it be before I see results?

If you perform the exercises that make up The Eigard Method correctly, your face will be sore the very next day. If you aren't sore, you probably aren't working the muscles hard enough. When you work your muscles until they "burn", meaning that you always sustain the exercise until the muscle is weak, you can expect to see the effects of your workouts within a couple of weeks.

How is The Eigard Method different from other facial exercise programs?

Most other exercise programs are like simple calisthenics and focus on one muscle at a time. Predictably, the results are hit-or-miss. By contrast, each exercise in The Eigard Method begins with a precise facial alignment, much like the basic positions in ballet, so that as you begin the exercise your whole face is engaged in a disciplined set of movements that build overall strength, posture, and control.

Some popular books on facial exercise offer advice that can be harmful. These books describe exercises that crease and pucker the delicate facial skin as you perform them, when it's well-known that repeated creasing is exactly what causes the collagen breakdown that leads to wrinkles. If you fan through the illustrations of The Eigard Method, you'll see a lot of funny-looking expressions, but not a single crease, pucker, or furrow.

Can I practice The Eigard Method even if I've had plastic surgery?

Cosmetic surgery patients can benefit tremendously from practicing The Eigard Method, either before or after their procedure. When surgery patients are dissatisfied with their results, it's often because the skin has been stretched tight while the muscle underneath continues to sag like an old rubber band, producing an unnatural rippled effect. The exercises in this book can help alleviate this condition by tightening the underlying muscle. Practiced before cosmetic surgery, The Eigard Method can give your doctor more to work with, improving your chances for a positive outcome. But physicians take heed: widespread use of The Eigard Method before surgery might result in a lot of cancelled appointments.

Does The Eigard Method work for men as well as for women?

You've probably noticed that men's and women's bodies respond to physical exercise in different ways. Because of their higher testosterone levels, men tend to build more bulk when they begin a weight-bearing exercise program than women do. The exercises in The Eigard Method, however, are designed to strengthen and tone muscle tissue and to build bulk only in areas where you want it—such as the cheeks. They are equally effective for men and women of any age.

Does The Eigard Method reverse sun damage?

When your sixth-grade teacher asked you to write an essay called "What I did on my summer vacation," you probably didn't write, "I ordered up some crow's-feet, but they won't be arriving for another twenty years." But maybe you should have. According to the American Academy of Dermatology, 80% of sun damage occurs before the age of eighteen. The Eigard Method will give you a fit face; still, it's never too late to prevent further sun damage—if you're forty now, you'll thank yourself at sixty. You should always wear a sunscreen with an SPF of at least 15. Read labels carefully, as many products sold as sunscreens do not block the full spectrum of UVA, UVB, and UVC rays. Adults who do wear sunscreen often forget that snow, water, and even pavement can reflect up to 80% of the sun's rays, burning the skin even in inclement weather. The good news is that you can take steps to minimize further damage even if you do accidentally burn. The damage from any burn continues to worsen over a twenty-four-hour period. To draw away the heat and arrest the damage, take a tepid bath. Since burns strip the skin of its protective mantle, mix a quart of cider vinegar into the bath water to restore your skin's pH balance. (Don't worry, the vinegar evaporates from your skin, and you won't come out smelling like a salad as long as you leave out the garlic and olive oil.)

Can I do these exercises in the car?

The exercises you will learn in The Eigard Method require a high level of concentration and precision. Distracted driving is dangerous, and distracted exercise is just plain useless. You also must ask yourself whether an exercise regimen easy enough to be performed while driving a car could possibly be rigorous enough to provide you with noticeable benefits.

Will I have to make funny faces for the rest of my life?

After you've trained your muscles in The Eigard Method, they will benefit from something called "muscle memory." This means that once you've achieved the results you want, you can go ahead and cut back on your program without fear of permanently losing the benefit of all that hard work. If you like, you can revert to a maintenance schedule of a few exercises several times a week. When you feel your muscles are ready for a new challenge, you can pick up the pace and take your program to a higher level.

As with any exercise program, the first hurdle is the biggest. Once you've made a good beginning, you'll be able to maintain your fitness level without undue suffering, and achieving higher levels of fitness will always be easier than that first big push. Yes, The Eigard Method requires you to do some work, but in return it offers a long-term benefit. That simply isn't true of a surgical face-lift. Remember, the younger you are when you start the program, the more memory your muscles will have.

Getting to Know Your Face

Before we begin the program, let's spend a moment discussing the basic structure of your face. You need to know the location of each muscle and the direction in which it is worked in order to prevent injury. As you read this section, refer to the diagram. The red arrows indicate the direction in which the muscles should be worked. When massaging a muscle, always follow the direction of the arrow, and when working out with any kind of weight, even your fingertips, always apply force (resistance) in the direction of the arrow.

What, exactly, do muscles do? Very simply put, muscles move your body. Think of a drawbridge at the entrance to a castle, one that is raised and lowered by a rope. The rope that moves the drawbridge is like a muscle. When shortened, it pulls the drawbridge up; extended, it lets the drawbridge down. Even the muscles in your face operate on this basic principle. (Think of your eyelid as a drawbridge and you'll quickly "see" the analogy.)

This diagram illustrates the correct direction in which to stroke the muscles; stroking contrary to these arrows will break down the tissue and can result in the stretching of both muscles and skin.

Origin and Insertion

Every muscle has two ends. The end of the muscle that is attached to the bone is called the point of *origin*. On the drawbridge, the rope's point of origin would be the castle wall where it is attached. The other end is called the point of *insertion*. This is the end of the muscle that grabs onto a moving part—either bone or soft tissue like a tendon.

When you look at your arm or leg muscles, it is relatively easy to tell origin from insertion. Generally, the point of origin will be closer to the core of the body, while the point of insertion will be farther away, attached to something that moves.

Let's look at an obvious example, your biceps (the muscle on your upper arm that bulges when you "flex" like Arnold Schwarzenegger). Sit in front of a table or desk and extend your right arm straight ahead. Keeping your arm straight, rest your hand on the table, palm facing upward. Let's pretend for the sake of argument that your arm is a drawbridge. An invading ant could use your arm to climb from the table to your shoulder, breaching your castle walls in a most ticklish and unwelcome manner.

So save yourself from invasion and close the drawbridge. Bend your arm at the elbow. Continue to bend it until your hand touches your shoulder. The drawbridge is closed. How, exactly, did that happen? Your brain sent a signal to your biceps, telling it to contract (shorten), moving your forearm up from the table. If you wanted to put your hand back on the table, all you'd have to do is send a neurological telegram telling the biceps to lengthen again.

Based on this model, can you tell which end of your biceps is the muscle's fixed point of origin? That's easy: the end that's attached to your shoulder. The other end moves your arm by attaching at the point of insertion on your forearm. Now you've got the idea.

Why is the concept of insertion/origin so important? Because you need to stroke the muscles in the proper direction—from insertion to origin—in order to keep from needlessly stretching the muscle and skin, which is exactly what happens when you massage a muscle in a contrary direction, or "against the grain." Too much stretching in the wrong direction can break down the tissue, resulting in muscles and skin that are "stretched out" like old rubber bands. As massage therapists learn when they study for their certification, always stroke from insertion to origin, never the other way around.

Finding the direction of your biceps was easy, but when it comes to the small muscles of your face, it's harder to tell which end is which. This is why you must study the diagram. Note that when you perform the warm up massage exercises, the muscles are all stroked from insertion to origin. By memorizing the sequence of massage strokes, you will learn the proper way to handle your face, whether you're exercising or taking off makeup.

Correcting Your Facial Posture

A face with perfect posture is a face without stress. It is relaxed and soft, neither tense nor slack. This doesn't mean that your face should be devoid of expression—quite the opposite. A stress-free face is the ideal tool for expressing the nuances of one's thoughts and feelings, guided by real emotion rather than force of habit. A relaxed face doesn't hold onto stale emotions but returns to a state of rest after it has performed its important work, ready for the next task.

Close your eyes and think of the people closest to you. Now begin to mentally catalog their characteristic facial expressions, many of which are not tools at all, but repetitive, unconscious habits: The best friend who smiles sideways to express irony or disdain. The boss whose clenched jaw means trouble with the board of directors. The husband who scowls when he reads. The mother who purses her lips just before any important pronouncement. These are the habits that eventually etch the face with lines and furrows that show one's age.

It's far easier to conjure up a mental image of the faces of your friends and relatives than it is to imagine your own because no matter how many hours a day you spend gazing at your lovely visage in the mirror, you almost never see your face in action. Later, when that vertical line appears on your forehead, you wonder how it got there, completely unaware that you furrow your brow every time you pause before answering a question at work.

Fortunately, bad habits can be broken through the following exercise.

To get a clear idea of just what your own facial habits are, arrange to keep a mirror next to the telephone on your desk or in your home. Really study your face as you listen and talk. Odds are, you will be surprised at what you see, including habits that you picked up from loved ones (your mother's pursed lips, your best friend's mouth twist). Don't worry at first about correcting yourself—take the time to observe closely.

When you've diagnosed yourself as a squinter, a jaw clencher, a scowler, or any combination thereof, then use the mirror to monitor yourself as you work to develop new habits.

Forehead: You may find that you scowl or frown at certain points during your conversation. To correct this habit, hold the palm of your hand lightly over your forehead. Your palm becomes your early-warning system: every time the muscles begin to bunch up in a frown, you will feel it happen and be reminded to keep them smooth.

Eyes: If you squint your eyes while thinking or if you wince frequently when you hear something unpleasant, practice letting your face and body react to the same stimulus without resorting to these habitual gestures. Also, if your crow's-feet come from squinting while driving to and from work, invest in a pair of good-quality sunglasses or have the windows of your car tinted.

Lips: Sometimes the best way to eliminate a bad habit is to replace it with a good one. If you're a lip purser by nature, use the mirror to practice keeping a slight smile on your face at all times. This smile will probably feel like a wide grin at first, but if you look in the mirror, you'll see that it's really just a relaxed, pleasant expression. Practice until this slight smile becomes the natural position of your face at rest.

Jaw: If you tend to clench your jaw while concentrating, introduce a new habit: let it fall loose and shake it out by moving it back and forth. This will release the pent-up tension in the muscles and bring you back to correct posture once again.

Remember, when your face is calm, you are calm.

LIFETIME FACIAL FITNESS WITHOUT PLASTIC SURGERY

Getting Started

Getting Started

Orientation

Always start your exercises with clean hands and a clean face. Wait until you're finished with your workout to apply any kind of cream or moisturizer so your face isn't slippery.

Before you begin, you will need a mirror and a straight-backed chair. The chair should be straight-backed because you can't achieve correct facial posture without correct body posture. When your body is lined up properly, your head and neck rest at a comfortable angle, free of stress and strain. Correct posture not only maximizes the benefits of your workout, it helps prevent injury.

> **Tip:**
>
> Your epidermis renews itself completely every thirty days. That's how long it takes a newly formed skin cell to migrate through the five layers of the epidermis and be sloughed off in the course of bathing, dressing, exercising, or just sitting reading a book. (Taken from biorap.org and medterms.com)

Body Alignment

The rule of thumb here is to keep six feet on the ground at all times. Two of the feet are yours, and the other four belong to the chair you are sitting in.

Sit up straight, your body at a ninety-degree angle to your legs.

Make sure your hips are pushed all the way back in the chair.

Your feet should be flat on the floor and parallel to each other.

Lift your shoulders in an exaggerated shrug, roll them back, then let them fall. This will put your body into the correct position. If your hands fall naturally into your lap, you're all set.

The Mirror: Your Assistant Coach

While the straight-backed chair is essential for good posture, don't try to learn these exercises without a mirror. Total facial discipline is essential to your success, and to achieve it, you need to know immediately when your face strays out of alignment. Beginning students make all sorts of strange, extraneous movements. For example, while concentrating on the forehead, many people unconsciously make odd movements with their mouths. How will you know you're making unconscious movements unless you can see them? Let the mirror be your assistant coach, showing you how you are doing. A wall-hung mirror is best. You don't want to have to look down, or up, to see your reflection.

If you wear glasses or contact lenses, you need to remove them prior to performing any of the eye exercises. If you can't see the mirror well enough to tell how you're doing, ask a friend to coach you a few times, or do the exercises with a buddy at first.

A Note on Breathing

Pay attention to your breathing as you work out. The flow of breath is important to any workout routine. As you inhale, you are taking in fresh oxygen to be carried in the bloodstream. As you exhale, you are eliminating contaminants (free radicals), which have the potential to age every inch of your body. A single breath does all this. Remember to breathe slowly and steadily as you continue with the program. Beginning students often focus so intensely on the exercises that they forget to breathe in and out. Normal breathing is key.

Duration

You'll notice that the instructions for each exercise tell you to repeat the exercise until you feel your muscles burn. This is very important. If you don't work the muscles until they tingle or quiver, you won't be making progress. Some people will need more repetitions to reach this level of exertion than others.

The Basic Set Positions: The Soft Face

Most of the beginning exercises start with a basic facial position called the soft face. This face is completely relaxed. It's blank. If you've ever had a passport photo taken, this is probably the face that was captured on film. Does it sound easy? It's not. Most adults carry some amount of tension in their facial muscles most of the time, even in sleep. Did you ever watch children sleep and notice how unusually angelic their faces appeared? That's because a child's face is truly relaxed in sleep.

A good way to get ready for the beginning level exercises is to practice releasing one facial muscle at a time.

Assume the Correct Position

Relax your forehead. Think of cool water from a tropical fountain beating down on it, washing it smooth in all directions.

Relax your eyes. Think of having a glazed look, staring ahead without effort.

Relax your mouth. If your jaw is clenched, let it fall slack. Your lips should be closed, your teeth slightly apart. Let your cheeks melt along with your mouth into complete smoothness.

The Basic Set Positions: The Hard Face

All of the advanced exercises in The Eigard Method use elements of the hard face. The hard face is designed to tense each and every muscle in the face simultaneously without wrinkling the skin.

While you work on the beginning exercises, take some time to practice the hard face all by itself. You'll find that it's tough to put all of the separate elements together, but by the time you're ready to move on to the advanced exercises, you should be able to perform all of the different components of the hard face simultaneously.

Assume the Correct Position

Tighten all the muscles of your face without wrinkling the skin.

Flatten your lips against your teeth, keeping them full and pressed together.

Slightly extend your jaw, while pressing upward with the corners of your lips. First your teeth should meet, then your lower teeth should extend slightly forward, still covered by your full, flat lips.

Extend your lower lip outward in a slight pout by pressing upward with your chin. Can you feel it in your neck?

Push upward with your lower eyelid muscles. Keep your upper eyelids open and your forehead smooth.

Stretch your tongue toward the top of your mouth. Curl it back so that the bottom of your tongue touches the roof of your mouth, and keep it back toward your throat.

Flare your nostrils.

Hold this position for ten seconds. Pat all over your face with your fingertips. It should feel hard all over if you're doing the position correctly.

Release. Shake out your muscles.

Repeat.

Neck and Jaw Area

Have you ever seen a woman whose elaborate hairdo looks fantastic from the front, but the back view looks like a good place to raise baby chicks? Her mistake is in believing that what you see—in the mirror—is what you get.

While it's true that mirrors never lie, they also never tell you the whole truth. That is because the mirror you gaze into every morning and every night shows you a two-dimensional version of the fairest of them all (you, of course), while the you that everyone else sees is a three-dimensional being. If you could see your own profile every day the way others do, you'd probably take this book to bed with you every night until you had memorized every workout.

In Beverly Hills, plastic surgery spotting is as much a sport as birdwatching is in other locales. One easy way of spotting a face-lift has always been to look for a person with a tight face and a loose, crepe-textured neck. And face-lift patients aren't alone: even the most health and beauty conscious among us often neglect the neck. Yet without good muscle tone in this area, the entire face will eventually take on an atrophied, sagging appearance. Our muscles begin to thin and weaken at a surprisingly young age—as early as twenty-five, when we reach our growth apex. This quite natural decline can be countered by the exercises in The Eigard Method, which can help build an elegant profile at any age.

The first three exercises in the program will make you aware of the neck's true purpose: to foster good facial posture. The Neck Lift (No. 1) will strengthen the neck muscles, improving overall posture. The King Tut (No. 2) (named for its mummylike hand position) concentrates on the jawline for tighter jowls, and the Chin Up (No. 3) will erase your double chin.

So start early, and keep your chin up. A loose, baggy neck and chin can easily be corrected, or avoided altogether, by practicing these exercises.

Cheek and Lip Area

Have you ever seen an actress on television who has had too many collagen shots? It's easy to spot. Too much collagen in the lips can make an otherwise attractive woman look like a platypus.

For kissable lips at any age, The Eigard Method targets the muscles that, when stimulated, plump up the lips naturally. Some students of the method have reported that their lips are the first feature to respond to their new workout, looking more pouty and full after just two weeks at the beginning level.

As for the cheeks, few people realize that these can give away your age at a glance. Have you ever seen a photograph of a beloved relative's profile? It's not difficult to gauge how old someone was when the photo was taken, just by noting the fullness in the cheeks. If you think about it, cheeks represent over half the area of the face, and the muscles have a tendency to become loose and elongated over time.

If left to nature, lips, too, tend to give away one's true age. Bad facial habits play a role: deep vertical grooves form after repeated pursing of the lips, a problem that's especially pronounced for smokers. But the passage of time also takes its toll: one of the onset signs of menopause is the thinning of the upper lip, resulting in lips that appear to fall into the mouth, for that denture look without the dentures. The Eigard Method will retrain and firm the muscles, which will lift the lips out of the mouth and soften the unsightly lines around them. Your lips will be as smooth and voluptuous as rose petals again, while your cheeks will grow as firm as winter apples.

Exercise No. 4, the Lip Up, will help keep your lips full and well defined. The Marionette (No. 5) strengthens the lower cheek area, for high-definition features. The Lip Press (No. 6) works to erase those fine vertical lines, while the Cheek Enhancer (No. 7) works the upper cheek area for a well-defined, high-cheekboned look.

Eyelid and Forehead Areas

Have you ever heard that the eyes are the windows to the soul? If that's the case, a lot of beautiful souls are peeking out from behind a curtain of puffy, creased, unsightly window-dressing. Are you one of them? The Eigard Method will help you tackle that remodeling project and give your soul a new view. You won't need to nip and tuck in order to get luxurious, velvety-smooth and crease-free eyelids.

The skin around the eye area is some of the most delicate skin anywhere on your body, yet it takes an incredible beating. Your eyes are constantly exposed to the elements, battered daily by sun and wind. They twist and turn every time you squint or smile and stretch to the breaking point as you scrub off your makeup. Still, it seems that some people get fine lines around their eyes at a very young age. Is it because they're carrying the woes of the world on their shoulders? Not necessarily.

A great deal of the eye's appearance is dictated by genetics, and muscle weakness around the eye can occur at any age. Some people naturally develop deeply creased and sagging upper eyelids or dark undereye circles, while others have more fatty tissue under their eyes than they'd like. All of these types will feel they look tired even when they've slept like a baby. In some cases, severely overhanging eyelids must be surgically corrected (insurance will pay for this procedure since it's a bona fide medical condition). But for most of us, the problem is merely cosmetic.

Whatever your genetic predisposition, you can get a lift by practicing the exercises in this section and developing your eyes' muscle memory. By firming up the underlying muscles, your eyelids will grow tighter and firmer, counteracting your DNA's handiwork as well as, or better than, expensive surgery.

Blepharoplasty, or eyelid surgery, costs from $2,000 to $12,000. Complications from any cosmetic surgery may be rare, but when they do occur they can be devastating. Remember, this is your eye area. How would you like to end up with eyes that won't close, blocked tear ducts, or tears that won't stop flowing? These disasters have happened to patients who underwent surgery simply to "brighten" their appearance. With The Eigard Method you'll experience no downtime and no downside.

The Lid Up (No. 8) will firm and smooth the undereye area, while Heavy Lids (No. 9) will keep your upper eyelids high and tight. Last but not least, the Brow Raiser (No. 10) will give you a smooth, clear, untroubled forehead.

Warm Up
Exercises

Warm Up Exercises

3

This series of warm up moves should be done in sequence. The massaging action stimulates the muscles, nerves, and skin on your face and neck by increasing the flow of oxygen through the blood and prepares them to receive maximum benefit from your workout. You won't get as much benefit from the exercises if you start them "cold." For maximum synergy, take the time to do the warm up exercise massage before you begin your exercises each day.

Though the body alignment described below is recommended, feel free to vary the routine to suit your lifestyle. For example, you might want to do your warm up exercise massage first thing in the morning, then do your exercises, and end with a cool down exercise massage as you apply your daily moisturizer. Use your imagination. Having a "perfect" exercise routine is useless if it's so inconvenient for you to follow that you never seem to get to it.

Always wash your hands and face before beginning the warm up exercise massage. For correct body alignment, you need to lie on a bed.

Tip:

Stress and tension activate the body's adrenal glands, causing blood vessels to constrict and deprive your skin of oxygen; without oxygen, your skin will wrinkle prematurely. (Taken from www.syence.com)

Warm Up Exercise Arrow Diagram

This diagram illustrates the correct direction as well as the suggested sequence in which to stroke the muscles: always from insertion to origin.

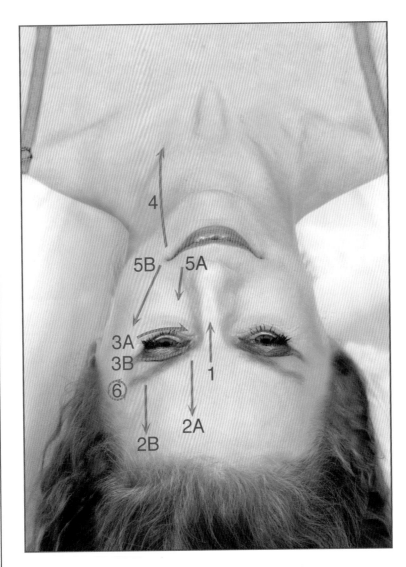

1. Nose: Stroke downward

2. Forehead: Stroke upward

3. Eyes: Pat gently

4. Chin/Neck: Stroke downward

5. Cheeks: Stroke upward

6. Temples: Stroke counterclockwise

Assume the Correct Position

Body Alignment

Lie on your back with your knees bent so the small of your back is in contact with the mattress at all times.

Hang your head slightly over the edge of the bed. Don't overdo it. Start with your head and neck flat on the bed, then inch your body toward the edge of the bed just until your neck begins to bend. Make sure the edge of the bed supports the nape of your neck.

Remain in this position for ten minutes while you do your warm up exercise massage.

Facial Alignment

During the exercise massage, your face should stay soft and relaxed.

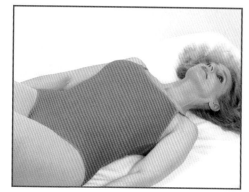
Body Alignment

Nose and Eyebrow Exercise

Place the tips of your index fingers at the bridge of your nose between your eyebrows.

Make several short downward strokes halfway down your nose, alternating fingers.

Repeat the motion on each side of your nose, under your inner eyebrow.

Repeat the sequence three times.

Nose and Eyebrow A

Nose and Eyebrow B

Forehead Exercise

Begin at the left side of your forehead, above the eyebrow, and stroke upward toward your hairline.

Use the entire flat side of your two middle fingers to make long, upward strokes.

Alternating your hands, move across your forehead to the right side.

Repeat the sequence three times.

Forehead A

Forehead B

Forehead C

Forehead D

Eye Area Exercise

Place the tips of your two middle fingers at the outer corners of your eyes.

Gently pat along the bony ridges of your eye sockets, under your eyes, working toward the inner corners.

Repeat, patting along the upper ridges of your eye sockets, again moving inward.

Repeat the sequence three times.

Outer Eye

Under Eye

Upper Eye

Chin and Neck Exercise

Use the four fingers on each hand like soft paddles.

Smile slightly toward the right, tightening the muscles around your mouth, chin, and neck.

Using your right hand, make several long, gentle downward strokes on the left side of your face and neck, working from the corner of your mouth to your collarbone.

Repeat for the left side of your face.

Repeat the sequence three times.

Chin and Neck A

Chin and Neck B

Cheek Exercise

Smile slightly, tightening the mouth area just enough to define your cheek muscles.

Hold your arms so that your forearms and hands are parallel to your chest.

Place three fingers (ring, middle, and index) of each hand beside each nostril, just below the flare of your cheek.

Slide your fingers up toward the inner corners of your eyes.

Next, place the same three fingers above the corners of your mouth.

Slide your fingers up toward the apex of each cheekbone—this is the highest point of the cheekbone, which lies just under the outer corner of your eye.

Repeat the sequence three times.

Inner Cheek A

Inner Cheek B

Outer Cheek A

Outer Cheek B

Temple Exercise

For this final movement, move your body so that your head is again lying flat on the bed.

Use your two middle fingers to massage your temples in a slow, counterclockwise direction. Use firm pressure.

Repeat the sequence three times.

Temple

Tip:

After you have finished your warm up exercises, sit up slowly. It's a good idea to sit on the edge of the bed for a moment or two before standing. You don't want to get dizzy.

Beauty is a form of genius—
is higher, indeed, than genius, as it
needs no explanation. It is of the great
facts in the world like sunlight, or
springtime, or the reflection in dark
water of that silver shell we call
the moon.

—*Oscar Wilde*

Beginning Exercises

4

Beginning Exercises

The beginning-level exercises in this book are designed to start you out on the road to facial fitness with a simple, stripped-down version of The Eigard Method. Think of these ten moves as the method with training wheels. By mastering them, you will be gaining the basic muscle control necessary to reap the full benefits of the advanced program.

All of these exercises begin with the "soft face" described in the orientation, a relaxed, peaceful facial posture in which all tension is drained from the face. As you begin your workout, be careful to tighten only the muscles involved in the exercise you're working on. Remember that if you crease your forehead in concentration while executing a Lip Up, you're defeating the whole purpose of the program.

As with any exercise program, be it Jane Fonda's or jujitsu, no pain means no gain. Always sustain the exercise until the muscles involved begin to burn. If you're wondering what this feels like, think about the last time you laughed until your face hurt. If you push yourself all the way, you'll wake up tomorrow to the first sign of true progress—a sore face.

NECK & JAWLINE AREA

Neck Lift

Level: **BEGINNING**

Area Worked: **NECK & JAWLINE**

Type of Exercise: **ISOTONIC/ISOMETRIC**

If you want to look good, you have to stick your neck out—literally. This exercise lays a firm foundation for strengthening the neck muscles. If you've ever suffered from neck pain due to a whiplash injury, improper work habits, or poor sleeping posture, this exercise can really help you.

This is the only one of the ten exercises in this book that isn't performed sitting in a straight-backed chair: For the Neck Lift, you need to lie down on either the floor or your bed. The body, face, and hand alignments remain the same for both forward- and side-facing positions.

Tip:

Unlike a sit-up, this is a very small movement. Your head should barely clear the floor. Keep your abdominal muscles firm, using them to press your back to the floor, but let your neck muscles, not your abs, do all the heavy lifting.

Caution:

It's very important to keep your knees bent while lying on your back to prevent muscle strain. Do not arch your back at any time.

Assume the Correct Position

Body Alignment

Lie on a flat surface, either the floor or a bed.

Bend your knees so your back is lying flat.

Facial Alignment

Stare straight ahead with a relaxed expression.

Hand Alignment

Use your hands to form a "chin cup": Place the tips of your index fingers at your temples. Now, place the edge of these fingers and your hands along your jawline so that the entire edge of your fingers and palm outlines the lower half of your face. Keep your palms cupped in a megaphone shape. Don't fold your hands in toward your cheeks, as this will cause you to pull the skin.

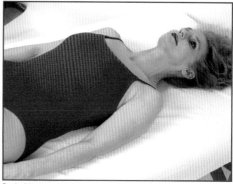
Body Alignment

Facial Alignment

Hand Alignment

Front-Facing Neck Lift

Resistance

With your head looking straight ahead, use your chin cup to apply steady pressure, pushing downward toward the floor or bed as you perform the following muscular contraction.

Muscular Contraction

Muscular Contraction

Gently raise your head off of the floor or bed, extending your jaw forward and resisting the movement by continuing to press downward with your chin cup.

Hold the contraction for ten seconds.

Release.

Repeat the exercise until your muscles feel the burn.

Side-Facing Neck Lift

Facial Alignment

Turn your head to the left side.

Hand Alignment

Use a one-handed chin cup on the right side of your face only.

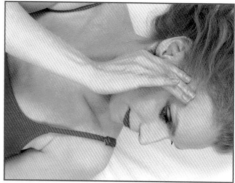

Hand Alignment

Resistance

Apply a steady, holding pressure. Push downward toward the floor or bed as you perform the following muscle contraction.

Muscular Contraction

Muscular Contraction

Gently raise your head off the bed or floor, extending your lower jaw forward and resisting the movement by continuing to press downward with your chin cup.

Hold the contraction for ten seconds.

Release.

Repeat the exercise until your muscles feel the burn.

Turn your head to the right and repeat the sequence.

Neck Lift Muscle Diagram

These are the muscles you should feel when you are doing this exercise.

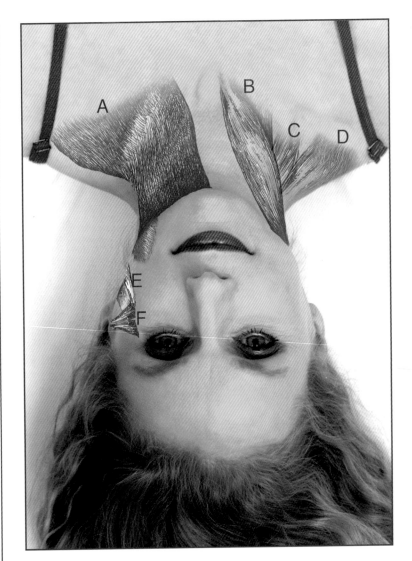

A. Platysma myodies

B. Sternocleidomastoid

C. Scalenus anterior

D. Trapezius (clavicular part)

E. Medial pterygoid

F. Lateral pterygoid

King Tut

Level: **BEGINNING**

Area Worked: **NECK & JAWLINE**

Type of Exercise: **ISOTONIC**

Our previous exercise concentrated primarily on strengthening the neck. Here we continue working the neck muscles, but incorporate the jowl area. These muscles, if not properly conditioned, can cause your jawline to droop over time.

The key to this exercise lies in natural mouth movements made unnatural by the addition of resistance. Remember, The Eigard Method is not based on repetition, but rather on precise, concentrated, and methodical execution. You should perform this exercise very slowly. It's a tough one.

Tip:

Are you feeling the pull? The resistance in this exercise is created by holding the front neck muscles firmly in place while stretching them. You hold them by placing your hands on them just above your collarbone. Try positioning your hands, then turn your face upward. Do you feel your neck muscles pull against your hands? If not, reposition your hands a bit higher, and try again. If you feel at all choked, then you are pushing too hard.

Assume the Correct Position

Hand Alignment

Cross your arms at the wrist and lay them on your chest, just like King Tut lying in his sarcophagus.

Tuck your thumbs toward the palms of your hands.

Place both hands firmly at the base of your neck, just above your collarbone.

Hand Alignment

Assume the Correct Position

Facial Alignment

Smile, widening your mouth.

Wrap your upper and lower lips over your teeth.

Resistance

Use your hands to hold the base of your neck muscle as you perform the exercise, *really feeling the pull against your hands.*

Muscular Contraction

Drop your lower jaw open as far as you can without unwrapping your lips.

Lift your jaw outward and then upward with a very slow scooping motion, trying to touch your nose with your lower lip.

Hold for five seconds.

Release.

Repeat the exercise until your muscles feel the burn.

Facial Alignment

Muscular Contraction A

Muscular Contraction B

King Tut Muscle Diagram

....

These are the muscles you should feel when you are doing this exercise.

A. Lateral pterygoid

B. Medial pterygoid

C. Orbicularis oris

D. Platysma myodies

UNDER CHIN & JAWLINE AREA

Chin Up

Level: **BEGINNING**

Area Worked: **UNDER CHIN & JAWLINE**

Type of Exercise: **ISOTONIC**

Some body parts look better in pairs, but the chin is not one of them. If you master this exercise, you will have no need for a surgical lift to correct your double chin.

The key here is that resistance is applied in both directions: while you open your mouth and while you close it. This wakes up those sleepy, little-used muscles under the chin.

3

Chin Up

Tip:
During this exercise, your jaw should be tense at all times, resisting in both directions.

Assume the Correct Position

Hand Alignment

With your palms facing each other, bend your fingers at a ninety-degree angle, overlapping them to form a "hand table." Now hold your hands under your chin.

Hand Alignment A

Facial Alignment

Smile wide, opening your mouth and extending your lower jaw forward.

Stretch your tongue toward the top of your mouth. Curl it back so that the bottom of your tongue touches the roof of your mouth.

Hand Alignment B

Resistance

Use your hand table to resist the downward movement of your jaw as you open your mouth. Then resist with your jaw as you push upward with your hand table to close your mouth.

Facial Alignment

3

Chin Up

Assume the Correct Position

Muscular Contraction

Open your mouth, forcing your jaw downward against your hand table.

Resisting with your jaw, slowly push your hand table up to close your mouth.

Hold each position (open and closed) for five seconds.

Release.

Repeat the exercise until your muscles feel the burn.

Muscular Contraction A

Muscular Contraction B

Chin Up Muscle Diagram

These are the muscles you should feel when you are doing this exercise.

A. Lateral pterygoid

B. Medial pterygoid

C. Supra-hyoid region:
   Digastric
   Stylo-hyoid
   Mylo-hyoid
   Genio-hyoid

Lip Up

Level: **BEGINNING**

Area Worked: **UPPER & LOWER LIP**

Type of Exercise: **ISOTONIC**

Here the lips are trained with consistent and precise movements. This is a two-part exercise, working first the upper and then the lower lip, with your fingers acting as dumbbells. The second part of the exercise in particular shortens and strengthens the area above the lip, resulting in the lip itself being lifted out of the mouth. You'll never need collagen injections.

When you finish performing your Lip Ups, your lips will feel like big balloons, ready to float right off your face. Don't worry, that's just what happens when you really get your blood moving. It's an uplifting experience.

Tip:

If your lips feel puffy and tingly after performing a few lip ups, you will know you're doing this exercise correctly.

4

Lip Up

Assume the Correct Position

Facial Alignment

Start with a slight smile.

Wrap your upper and lower lips over your teeth.

Facial Alignment A

Facial Alignment B

Upper Lip Workout

Hand Alignment

Hold your elbows out, your forearms parallel to the ground.

Place the sides of your index fingers flat along the upper edge of your upper lip, fingertips pointing at each other.

Resistance

Your index fingers are used as "finger dumbbells" in this exercise, providing spot-specific resistance.

Muscular Contraction

Roll your finger dumbbells by rotating your fingers as if to pull your top lip up and out of your mouth. Your fingernails will rotate away from your mouth.

Resist the rolling motion by pulling your upper lip back down and over your teeth.

Hold the contraction for five seconds.

Release.

Repeat the exercise until your muscles feel the burn.

Hand Alignment

Muscular Contraction

4

Lip Up

Lower Lip Workout

Hand Alignment

Hold your elbows out, your forearms parallel to the ground.

Place the sides of your index fingers flat along the lower edge of your lower lip, fingertips pointing at each other.

Resistance

Your index fingers are used as finger dumbbells in this exercise, providing spot-specific resistance.

Muscular Contraction

Roll your finger dumbbells by rotating your fingers toward your mouth. This will pull your lower lip down and out of your mouth.

Resist the rolling motion by pulling your lower lip back up and over your teeth.

Hold the contraction for five seconds.

Release.

Repeat the exercise until your muscles feel the burn.

Hand Alignment

Muscular Contraction

4

Lip Up

Lip Up Muscle Diagram

These are the muscles you should feel when you are doing this exercise.

A. Buccinator

B. Orbicularis oris

C. Risorius

The Marionette

Level: BEGINNING

Area Worked: LIPS & LOWER CHEEKS

Type of Exercise: ISOMETRIC

This exercise strengthens the lower cheek areas, the part of your face that is susceptible to smile lines, while giving a firm appearance to the mouth. An easy way to get your mouth into working position is to shout or sing the word "Peru" out loud and elongate the "u," and then hold the position. You should look a little bit like a goldfish. If you happen to have small children in the house, doing this exercise in front of them will keep them laughing. This exercise is called "the Marionette" because the best way to get the technique exactly right is by imagining that your lips are being controlled by a pair of strings.

Tip:

It helps to think of your elongated mouth as a rectangle, with strings attached at the upper lip and running to the corners of each nostril. Open and close your mouth by pulling up and down on these strings like you would on a marionette—just don't close your mouth all the way.

Assume the Correct Position

Facial Alignment

Flare out your lips like a fish, making a long, slightly square shape with your mouth. Imagine marionette strings running from the corners of your nostrils to the top of your upper lip.

Extend your jaw forward.

Facial Alignment

Resistance

This exercise uses only the natural resistance created by the muscular contraction.

Muscular Contraction

Push your lips forward by squeezing your cheeks together, narrowing the "O" of your mouth. Don't purse your lips! Keep them flared open and long. Most of the movement comes from the "strings" attached to the upper lip.

Hold for five seconds.

Return to the wide-open square. Do not let the corners of your mouth bow outward. Pull straight up on your marionette strings.

Hold the contraction for five seconds.

Release.

Repeat the exercise until your muscles feel the burn.

Muscular Contraction A

Muscular Contraction B

The Marionette Muscle Diagram

These are the muscles you should feel when you are doing
this exercise.

A. Orbicularis oris

B. Buccinator

UPPER LIP AREA

Lip Press

6

Level: **BEGINNING**

Area Worked: **UPPER LIP**

Type of Exercise: **ISOMETRIC**

This exercise is simple, but it's one you can feel right away. If you've stopped wearing bright shades of lipstick because they tend to bleed on you now that you're older, then the Lip Press is going to change your life. This exercise strengthens your upper lip and eliminates those fine vertical lines that make your lipstick feather. If you're too young to have experienced this phenomenon, you will love the Lip Press for giving you fuller lips than you imagined possible without surgery.

Tip:

Do not let your upper lip pucker during this exercise. To keep it from doing so, make sure that the resistance you supply with your fingers is equal to the outward pressure of your smile. The burn will come as you hold the position, not from excessive force.

Tip:

Your entire upper lip area should feel "hard" to the touch when you are in the proper position for this exercise.

Assume the Correct Position

Facial Alignment

Flatten your lips against your teeth, keeping them flat and pressed together.

Slightly extend your jaw while pressing upward with the corners of your lips.

Resistance

Place your "finger dumbbells"—the flat pads of your index fingers—just above the corners of your firm upper lip. Press gently inward, resisting the outward smile of your upper lip.

Muscular Contraction

Hold your upper lip in position (firm and full, smiling slightly) throughout the exercise.

Hold the contraction for five seconds.

Release.

Repeat the exercise until your muscles feel the burn.

Facial Alignment

Resistance

Lip Press Muscle Diagram

These are the muscles you should feel when you are doing
this exercise.

A. Orbicularis oris

Cheek Enhancer

Level: **BEGINNING**

Area Worked: **CHEEKS**

Type of Exercise: **ISOTONIC**

If you master this two-part exercise, you can have cheekbones like Katharine Hepburn's. This inner and outer cheek workout lifts the upper cheek area by building up those tired, lazy, and droopy muscles. Using an inventive hand movement, your fingers will supply support and resistance to the specific area as you continue to work the cheek muscles. This exercise uses the skills you learned in Exercise No. 5, the Marionette. We're adding resistance to give the upper cheek area a workout.

Tip:

Training yourself to sleep on your back is good for your skin, but it can also go a long way toward preventing neck problems. It's all part of good facial and body posture.

Assume the Correct Position

Facial Alignment

Flare your lips like a fish, making a long, slightly square shape with your mouth.

Extend your jaw forward.

Facial Alignment

Inner Cheek Workout

Hand Alignment

Raise your elbows up and out so that your hands rest in front of your face, fingers pointing downward.

Place your middle and ring fingers next to your nose, just below your tear ducts, holding the tops of the cheek muscles from above.

Hand Alignment

Resistance

As you perform the following muscular contraction, firmly hold your cheek muscles with your fingertips.

Muscular Contraction

Push your lips forward by squeezing your cheeks together, narrowing the "O" of your mouth. Resist the forward motion of your cheek muscles with pressure from your fingertips as you elongate your mouth.

Muscular Contraction

Hold the contraction for two seconds.

Release.

Repeat the exercise until your muscles feel the burn.

Outer Cheek Workout

Hand Alignment

Raise your elbows up and out so that your hands rest in front of your face, fingers pointing downward.

Place your middle and ring fingers, slightly separated, along the top edge of your cheekbones, below the outer corners of your eyes.

Resistance

As you perform the following muscular contraction, firmly hold your cheek muscles with your fingertips.

Muscular Contraction

Push your lips forward by squeezing your cheeks together, narrowing the "O" of your mouth. Resist the forward motion of your cheek muscles with pressure from your fingertips as you elongate your mouth.

Hold the contraction for two seconds.

Release.

Repeat the exercise until your muscles feel the burn.

Hand Alignment

Muscular Contraction

Cheek Enhancer Muscle Diagram

These are the muscles you should feel when you are doing this exercise.

A. Levator labii superioris alaequa nasi

B. Levator labii superioris

C. Zygomaticus minor

D. Zygomaticus major

E. Orbicularis oris

EYE AREA

Lid Up

8

Level: **BEGINNING**

Area Worked: **LOWER EYELIDS**

Type of Exercise: **ISOTONIC**

Robert Mitchum's droopy lower eyelids gave him a haunted, sexy magnetism in the film noir classics from the '50s. But for most of us, a tight, smooth undereye area is a far more practical and pleasant look, particularly for women. Unfortunately, women inadvertently do far more damage to their eyes than men because of all the tugging and stretching done to remove eye makeup. If you master the Lid Up, you can use it to "harden" the eye area while you take off your makeup. Remember to always stroke inward toward your nose.

Even if you don't wear mascara, Lid Ups will help you achieve a smooth, tight undereye area. The trick is to work your lower eyelids only, while keeping your forehead smooth and your eyes open.

Here you're learning to isolate the muscles under your eyes.

Tip:

If you're performing your Lid Ups correctly, you will feel the muscles that surround your eyes quiver with exertion.

Caution:

Remove contact lenses before performing this exercise!

Caution:

Fingernails long and sharp? Trim them, put on cotton gloves, or skip this exercise.

Lid Up

8

Assume the Correct Position

Hand Alignment

Raise your elbows so that your forearms are parallel to the ground.

Gently rest your hands on your forehead horizontally, fingertips just touching. Keep your elbows pointed out throughout the exercise to avoid dragging your skin downward.

Hand Alignment

Facial Alignment

Stare straight ahead with a relaxed expression.

Resistance

This exercise uses only the natural resistance created by the muscular contraction.

Muscular Contraction

Muscular Contraction

Push up with the lower eyelids only. The upper eyelids should stay open and the forehead should remain motionless. Don't squint. Your hands are there to help you catch any accidental movement in your brow. This takes some practice.

Hold for two seconds.

Release.

Repeat the exercise until your muscles feel the burn.

Lid Up Muscle Diagram

These are the muscles you should feel when you are doing this exercise.

A. Orbicularis
   oculi pars palebral

EYE AREA

Heavy Lids

Level: **BEGINNING**

Area Worked: **UPPER EYELIDS**

Type of Exercise: **ISOTONIC**

9

This exercise improves and prevents the double-lidded effect. You will literally be weightlifting with your eyelids, creating tighter muscles. These strong muscles will hold the upper lids up high despite gravity's every attempt to pull them down.

Tip:

If you see stars, you're pressing too hard.

Caution:

Remove contact lenses before you begin this exercise and use extremely gentle pressure.

Caution:

Fingernails long and sharp? Trim them, put on cotton gloves, or skip this exercise.

9

Heavy Lids

Assume the Correct Position

Facial Alignment

Close your eyes tightly and maintain a relaxed expression.

Hand Alignment

Raise your elbows so that your forearms are parallel to the ground.

Gently rest the tips of your middle fingers on the center of each upper eyelid.

Resistance

Resist the opening of your upper eyelids by holding with the firm but light touch of your middle fingers.

Muscular Contraction

Try to force your eyes to open. Work the eyelids only. Do not lift with the eyebrow muscles.

Hold the contraction for two seconds.

Release.

Repeat the exercise until your muscles feel the burn.

Facial Alignment

Hand Alignment

Muscular Contraction

9

Heavy Lids

Heavy Lids Muscle Diagram

These are the muscles you should feel when you are doing this exercise.

A. Levator palpebrae superioris

B. Orbicularis oculi pars palebral

Brow Raiser

10

Level: BEGINNING

Area Worked: EYEBROWS & FOREHEAD

Type of Exercise: ISOMETRIC

Targeting the vertical and horizontal lines of the forehead and ending with a brow-strengthener, these three moves will re-educate your muscles, training them to resist the creasing effect of frowning and furrowing. The end result? A smoother forehead.

Tip:

If you can feel the skin moving beneath your fingertips, apply more pressure.

We've saved this exercise for last, because it feels wonderful. Once you've learned how to do it in front of a mirror, this is a good exercise to do while sitting at your desk in the office. Remember your posture when you do it—but you always sit up straight at work, don't you? The Brow Raiser creates a sensation of opening in the forehead area for a wonderful sense of release and relief from stress.

Assume the Correct Position

The basic facial alignment for all three versions of the Brow Raiser is the same, though your hand placement will vary.

Facial Alignment

Stare straight ahead with a relaxed expression.

Facial Alignment

Brow Raiser

10

Vertical Line Workout

Hand Alignment

Raise your elbows so that your forearms are parallel to the ground.

Place the first three fingers of each hand horizontally across your forehead just above your eyebrows, fingertips horizontal and meeting in the middle.

Hand Alignment

Resistance

Apply outward and upward pressure with your fingers to hold your forehead firmly in place.

Muscular Contraction

Attempt to scowl, trying to force your eyebrows inward and together against the holding pressure of your hands.

Muscular Contraction

Hold the contraction for two seconds.

Release.

Repeat the exercise until your muscles feel the burn.

10

Brow Raiser

Horizontal Line Workout

Hand Alignment

Hold your hands in front of your face.

Place the tips of the first three fingers of each hand above your eyebrows with your fingertips pointing upward.

Resistance

With downward pressure from your fingers, hold your forehead firmly in place.

Muscular Contraction

As if you are surprised, force your eyebrow muscles upward against the holding pressure of your hands.

Hold the contraction for two seconds.

Release.

Repeat the exercise until your muscles feel the burn.

Hand Alignment

Muscular Contraction

10

Brow Raiser

Eyebrow Workout

Hand Alignment

Raise your elbows so that your forearms are parallel to the ground.

Fan all of your fingertips out along your whole forehead, just above your eyebrows, fingertips pointing downward and palms above your forehead.

Hand Alignment

Resistance

With upward pressure from your fingers, hold your forehead firmly in place.

Muscular Contraction

As if frowning, force your eyebrow muscles downward against the holding pressure of your hands.

Hold the contraction for two seconds.

Release.

Repeat the exercise until your muscles feel the burn.

Muscular Contraction

Brow Raiser Muscle Diagram

These are the muscles you should feel when you are doing this exercise.

A. Occipitofrontalis (frontal portion)

B. Corrugator supercilii

There is no cosmetic for beauty
like happiness.

—*Marguerite Gardiner Blessington*

Advanced Exercises

CHAPTER

5

Advanced Exercises

5

I f you are ready to move on to the exercises in this section, then you're about to experience a truly amazing transformation. As you gain proficiency in the advanced exercises, you'll discover that facial fitness isn't just about staying youthful. By taking your workout to the next level, you will be building higher, tighter cheekbones, fuller lips, and a more graceful jawline than you ever imagined possible. And unlike surgically enhanced features, those you are about to sculpt will belong to you, with the harmony of line and proportion that only the steady hand of nature can design.

The ten advanced exercises in this section form the core of The Eigard Method. Unlike the beginning exercises, which focus on one area of the face at a time, each of these master exercises involves the majority of the fifty-seven muscles of the face and neck. By hardening these muscles, each of these exercises becomes dynamic, a mini-full-face workout in itself. This is why, with The Eigard Method advanced exercises, you can maintain facial fitness by practicing a few exercises at a time between full workouts.

As you're about to learn, keeping tension in so many muscles at once requires a great deal of practice and control. If you've skipped ahead without attempting the beginning exercises, go ahead and try one or two of the advanced exercises right now, we'll wait for you. Back already? Did you feel like you were juggling, reciting Shakespeare, chewing gum, and knitting a sweater all at the same time? Don't despair. The Eigard Method is a challenging exercise program, and that's the reason it works so well. You can read through this book in an afternoon, but it's meant to last you a lifetime.

If you follow the program from the beginning, you'll always make progress and you'll never be bored. And by the time you're ready for the advanced exercises described in this section, you'll already be well on your way to facial fitness. Just remember that by mastering the advanced exercises, you may find yourself looking even better at fifty than you did at twenty.

NECK & JAWLINE AREA

Neck Lift

Level: **ADVANCED**

Area Worked: **NECK & JAWLINE**

Type of Exercise: **ISOTONIC/ISOMETRIC**

Just like the beginning Neck Lift, this exercise is repeated in both front- and side-facing positions. The body, face, and hand alignments remain the same. You are adding elements of the hard face set position.

While performing the advanced Neck Lift, your face will grow quite flushed. This is good for you. Increased circulation can go a long way toward improving the skin's general condition. In fact, a combination of exercise, increased fluid intake, plenty of sleep, and a healthy diet are your best weapons against unavoidable environmental factors such as air pollution and stress. The more of these you can manage to include in any given day, the healthier your skin will look and feel. So start your day with a few Neck Lifts before you get out of bed, and get a head start.

Assume the Correct Position

Body Alignment

Lie on a flat surface, either the floor or a bed.

Bend your knees so your back is lying flat.

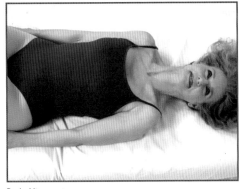

Body Alignment

Facial Alignment

Tighten all the muscles of your face without wrinkling the skin.

Flatten your lips against your teeth, keeping them full and pressed together.

Slightly extend your jaw, while pressing upward with the corners of your lips. First your teeth should meet, then your lower teeth should extend slightly forward, still covered by your full, flat lips.

Extend your lower lip outward in a slight pout by pressing upward with your chin. Can you feel it in your neck?

Push upward with your lower eyelid muscles. Keep your upper eyelids open and your forehead smooth.

Stretch your tongue toward the top of your mouth. Curl it back so that the bottom of your tongue touches the roof of your mouth, and keep pushing it back toward your throat.

Flare your nostrils.

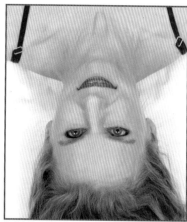

Facial Alignment

Hand Alignment

Hand Alignment

Use your hands to form a chin cup: place the tips of your index fingers at your temples. Now, place the edge of these fingers and your hands along the jawline so that the entire edge of your fingers and palm outlines the lower half of your face. Keep your palms cupped in a megaphone shape. Don't fold your hands in toward your cheeks, as this will cause you to pull the skin.

Front-Facing Neck Lift

Resistance

Looking straight ahead, use your chin cup to apply steady pressure, pushing downward toward the floor or bed as you perform the following muscular contraction.

Muscular Contraction

Muscular Contraction

Gently raise your head up, extending your jaw forward and resisting the movement by continuing to press downward with your chin cup.

Hold the contraction for ten seconds.

Release.

Repeat the exercise until your muscles feel the burn.

Tip:

Whiplash, anyone? Significant neck injury can arise from impact speeds as low as five miles per hour. Women suffer whiplash injury from car accidents twice as often as men do. This is one more good reason to build up those neck muscles. (Taken from J. Dolinis, "Risk Factors for 'Whiplash' in Drivers: A Cohort Study of Rear-End Traffic Crashes," *Injury* (1977): 173–179)

Side-Facing Neck Lift

Facial Alignment

Turn your head to the left side.

Hand Alignment

Use a one-handed chin cup on the right side of your face only.

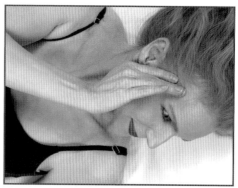
Hand Alignment

Resistance

Apply a steady, holding pressure. Push downward toward the floor or bed as you perform the following muscle contraction.

Muscular Contraction

Gently raise your head up, extending your lower jaw forward and resisting the movement by continuing to press downward with your chin cup.

Muscular Contraction

Hold the contraction for ten seconds.

Release.

Repeat the exercise until your muscles feel the burn.

Turn your head to the right and repeat the sequence.

Neck Lift Muscle Diagram

These are the muscles you should feel when you are doing this exercise.

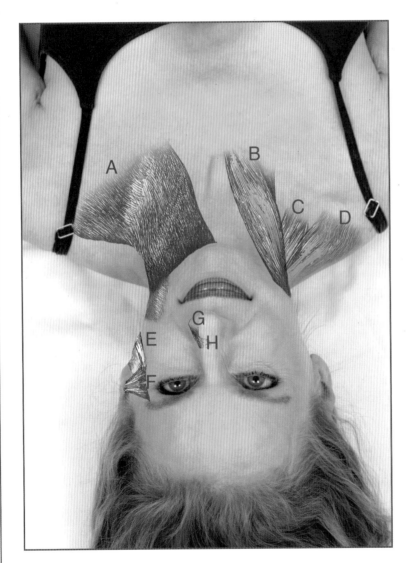

A. Platysma myodies

B. Sternocleidomastoid

C. Scalenus anterior

D. Trapezius (clavicular part)

E. Medial pterygoid

F. Lateral pterygoid

G. Dilator naris posterior

H. Dilator naris anterior

King Tut

Level: **ADVANCED**

Area Worked: **NECK & JAWLINE**

Type of Exercise: **ISOTONIC**

King Tut

By adding elements of the hard face, this exercise becomes much tougher to perform than the beginning version. Getting all of the elements to come together takes some practice, but keep working at it and you'll get that "aha" feeling when everything falls into place. The addition of the tongue curl makes this exercise a very deep workout for the neck, getting right to those underlying muscles—the ones you never knew you had until they begin to ache from this workout.

Assume the Correct Position

Hand Alignment

Cross your arms at the wrist and lay them on your chest, just like King Tut lying in his sarcophagus.

Tuck your thumbs toward the palms of your hands.

Place both hands firmly at the base of your neck, just above your collarbone.

Hand Alignment

Facial Alignment

Smile, widening your mouth.

Wrap your upper and lower lips over your teeth.

Stretch your tongue toward the top of your mouth. Curl it back so that the bottom of your tongue touches the roof of your mouth, and keep pushing it back toward your throat.

Extend your jaw forward, leading with your chin and keeping your mouth open wide.

Push up with your lower eyelids.

Flare your nostrils.

Resistance

Tilt your head back to create a tight neck muscle. Really feel the pull against your hands.

Facial Alignment

Resistance

Muscular Contraction

Lift your jaw outward and then upward with a very slow scooping motion, trying to touch your nose with your lower lip. Don't forget to keep curling your tongue back toward your throat.

Hold for five seconds.

Release.

Repeat the exercise until your muscles feel the burn.

Muscular Contraction

Tip:

Remember your first aerobics class or the first time you put on a pair of running shoes? You may feel just as clumsy and awkward in your first few sessions using The Eigard Method. This is because you are consciously working muscles that have never been given a true workout.

King Tut Muscle Diagram

These are the muscles you should feel when you are doing this exercise.

A. Masseter

B. Zygomaticus major

C. Dilator naris anterior

D. Dilator naris posterior

E. Lateral pterygoid

F. Medial pterygoid

G. Orbicularis oris

H. Platysma myodies

Chin Up

EXERCISE

3

> Level: **ADVANCED**
>
> Area Worked: **UNDER CHIN & JAWLINE**
>
> Type of Exercise: **ISOTONIC**

If you can do the hard face with ease, the advanced Chin Up will be a snap. Like the beginning version, it will help keep your chin tight and defined. The difference here is that this advanced version gives the whole face a workout, as do the advanced versions of all ten of the exercises in The Eigard Method. This means that even if you only performed this one exercise every day, your entire face would benefit. The advanced exercises may be difficult, but mastering them gives you unlimited freedom to customize your workout to suit your busy schedule.

Assume the Correct Position

Hand Alignment

With your palms facing each other, bend your fingers at a ninety-degree angle, overlapping the fingers to form a hand table. Now hold your hands under your chin.

Hand Alignment

Facial Alignment

Tighten all the muscles of your face without wrinkling the skin.

Flatten your lips against your teeth, keeping them full and pressed together.

Push upward with your lower eyelid muscles. Keep your upper eyelids open and your forehead smooth.

Stretch your tongue toward the top of your mouth. Curl it back so that the bottom of your tongue touches the roof of your mouth, and keep pushing it back toward your throat.

Now smile wide, opening your mouth and extending your lower jaw forward. Keep the lips full and flat.

Facial Alignment

Resistance

Use your hand table to resist the downward movement of your jaw as you open your mouth. Then resist with your jaw as you push upward with your hand table to close the mouth.

Resistance

Muscular Contraction

Open your mouth, forcing your jaw downward against your hand table.

Resisting with your jaw, slowly push your hand table up to close your mouth.

Hold each position (open and closed) for five seconds.

Release.

Repeat the exercise until your muscles feel the burn.

Muscle Contraction

Tip:

When the body is dehydrated, salivary glands compensate by producing more saliva to facilitate chewing and digestion. Blood vessels become "leaky" in order to supply the salivary glands with water to manufacture saliva. The "leakiness" causes increased bulk under the skin of the chin, cheeks, and neck. (Taken from www.water-cure2.com)

Chin Up Muscle Diagram

These are the muscles you should feel when you are doing this exercise.

A. Masseter

B. Zygomaticus major

C. Dilator naris anterior

D. Dilator naris posterior

E. Lateral pterygoid

F. Medial pterygoid

G. Supra-hyoid region:
Digastric
Stylo-hyoid
Mylo-hyoid
Genio-hyoid

Lip Up

Level: **ADVANCED**

Area Worked: **UPPER & LOWER LIP**

Type of Exercise: **ISOTONIC**

In this advanced version of the Lip Up, you're going to harden your facial muscles to make the workout more intense. Then, if you think you're ready, you can tackle the full lip workout, which uses a three-part hand motion. The facial alignment for each part of the exercise remains the same.

Tip:

Smokers get more wrinkles than nonsmokers. Yes, smoking decreases blood flow to the skin, and nicotine depletes the body's store of vitamin C. But smoker's mouth, characterized by fine vertical creases all around the lips, is a direct result of the repetitive puckering motion made while smoking.

4

Lip Up

Assume the Correct Position

Facial Alignment

Tighten all the muscles of your face without wrinkling the skin.

Flatten your lips against your teeth, keeping them full and pressed together.

Slightly extend your jaw, while pressing upward with the corners of your lips. First your teeth should meet, then your lower teeth should extend slightly forward, still covered by your full, flat lips.

Extend your lower lip outward in a slight pout by pressing upward with your chin. Can you feel it in your neck?

Push upward with your lower eyelid muscles. Keep your upper eyelids open and your forehead smooth.

Stretch your tongue toward the top of your mouth. Curl it back so that the bottom of your tongue touches the roof of your mouth, and keep pushing it back toward your throat.

Flare your nostrils.

Smile slightly.

Wrap your upper and lower lips over your teeth.

Facial Alignment A

Facial Alignment B

4

Lip Up

Upper Lip Workout

Hand Alignment

Hold your elbows out with your forearms parallel to the ground.

Place the sides of your index fingers flat along the upper edge of your upper lip, fingertips pointing at each other.

Resistance

Your index fingers are used as finger dumbbells in this exercise, providing spot-specific resistance.

Muscular Contraction

Roll your finger dumbbells by rotating your fingers, as if to pull your top lip up and out of your mouth. Your fingernails will rotate away from your mouth.

Resist the rolling motion by pulling your upper lip back down and over your teeth.

Hold the contraction for five seconds.

Release.

Repeat the exercise until your muscles feel the burn.

Hand Alignment

Muscular Contraction

4

Lip Up

Lower Lip Workout

Hand Alignment

Hold your elbows out with your forearms parallel to the ground.

Place the sides of your index fingers flat along the lower edge of your lower lip, fingertips pointing at each other.

Hand Alignment

Resistance

Your index fingers are used as finger dumbbells in this exercise, providing spot-specific resistance.

Muscular Contraction

Roll your finger dumbbells by rotating your fingers toward your mouth. This will pull your lower lip down and out of your mouth.

Muscular Contraction

Resist the rolling motion by pulling your lower lip back up and over your teeth.

Hold the contraction for five seconds.

Release.

Repeat the exercise until your muscles feel the burn.

Full Lip Workout—Part 1

The following is a three-part continuous movement. Instead of holding the positions, you keep moving from one to the other.

Resistance

Place your finger dumbbells flat along your upper lip.

Muscular Contraction

Keep your upper lip firm while resisting an upward and outward rolling motion of your finger dumbbells.

Muscular Contraction

4

Lip Up

Full Lip Workout—Part 2

Resistance

Place the tips of your index fingers one at each corner of your mouth, keeping your slight smile.

Muscular Contraction

Pull slightly outward on each corner of your mouth, first right, then left, then both together. Resist the outward pull of your fingers by contracting your lip muscles.

Muscular Contraction A

Muscular Contraction B

Muscular Contraction C

Full Lip Workout—Part 3

Resistance

Place your finger dumbbells flat along your lower lip.

Muscular Contraction

Keep your lower lip firm while resisting a downward and outward rolling motion from your finger dumbbells.

Release.

Repeat the sequence until your muscles feel the burn.

Muscular Contraction

4

Lip Up

Lip Up Muscle Diagram

These are the muscles you should feel when you are doing this exercise.

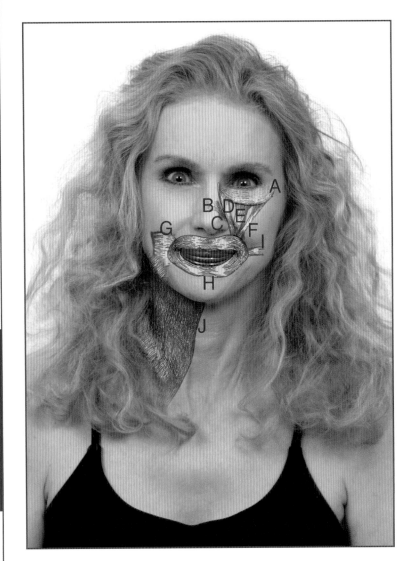

A. Orbicularis oculi

B. Dilator naris anterior

C. Dilator naris posterior

D. Levator labii superioris alaequa nasi

E. Levator labii superioris

F. Zygomaticus minor

G. Buccinator

H. Orbicularis oris

I. Risorius

J. Platysma myodies

The Marionette

Level: **ADVANCED**

Area Worked: **LIPS & LOWER CHEEKS**

Type of Exercise: **ISOMETRIC**

During this version of the Marionette, keep the tension in your cheeks at all times, both during the muscle contraction and as you release. If you relax the muscles between contractions, the corners of your lips will bow outward. Your lips should always be in a fish-like "O"— don't become a wide-mouthed frog.

Caution:

If your finger dumbbells slip down to rest too low (where the corners of your mouth would be if you were smiling) your lips will be stretched too wide. Keep those corners straight up and down as you move your mouth, as if they are being held in place by rods.

Assume the Correct Position

Facial Alignment

Flare out your lips like a fish, making a long, slightly square shape with your mouth. Imagine marionette strings running from the corners of your nostrils to the top of your upper lip.

Extend your jaw forward.

Push up with your lower eyelids. Force your upper eyelids to stay open and keep your forehead smooth.

Facial Alignment

Assume the Correct Position

Hand Alignment

Insert your index fingers into your mouth with your palms facing together. Keep your fingers stiff and straight. Rest them just above—not in—the corners of your mouth.

Resistance

Keep your cheek muscles tight while exerting outward pressure with your fingers. Keep your fingers straight and parallel.

Muscular Contraction

Try to push your fingers back together by tightening your cheek muscles. Remember not to purse your lips.

Hold the contraction for five seconds.

Release.

Repeat the exercise until your muscles feel the burn

Hand Alignment

Muscular Contraction

Tip:

Those muscle stimulating devices for sale on late-night television infomercials are very dangerous. If misplaced even slightly, the electrical stimulator can induce sharp muscle contractions that work the muscle in the wrong direction and cause damage.

The Marionette Muscle Diagram

These are the muscles you should feel when you are doing this exercise.

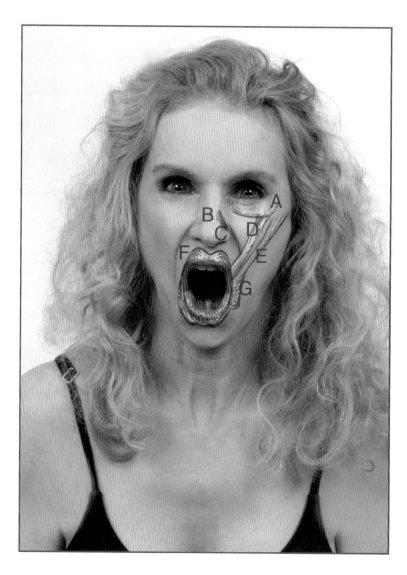

A. Orbicularis oculi

B. Dilator naris anterior

C. Dilator naris posterior

D. Zygomaticus minor

E. Zygomaticus major

F. Orbicularis oris

G. Buccinator

Lip Press

Level: ADVANCED

Area Worked: UPPER LIP

Type of Exercise: ISOMETRIC

The advanced Lip Press is like the bench press of facial fitness; it's a power move that is as fun to do as it is rewarding. Once you've had some practice with this one, you can increase both fingertip pressure and duration, going for an intense burn.

Tip:

The collagen layer in the skin tends to thin as we age. Don't bother spending money on those collagen-rich wrinkle creams—the collagen molecule is too large to penetrate the dermis (skin). Try eating gelatin, which is made from animal collagen, or taking vitamin C. (Taken from the Protein Data Bank at www.rcsb.org/pdb.)

Assume the Correct Position

Facial Alignment

Tighten all the muscles of your face without wrinkling the skin.

Flatten your lips against your teeth, keeping them full and pressed together.

Slightly extend your jaw, while pressing upward with the corners of your lips. First your teeth should meet, then your lower teeth should extend slightly forward, still covered by your full, flat lips.

Facial Alignment

Assume the Correct Position

Facial Alignment

Extend your lower lip outward in a slight pout by pressing upward with your chin. Can you feel it in your neck?

Push upward with your lower eyelid muscles. Keep your upper eyelids open and your forehead smooth.

Stretch your tongue toward the top of your mouth. Curl it back so that the bottom of your tongue touches the roof of your mouth, and keep pushing back toward your throat.

Flare your nostrils.

Resistance

Resistance

Place your finger dumbbells—the flat pads of your index fingers—just above the corners of your firm upper lip. Press gently inward, resisting the outward smile of the upper lip.

Muscular Contraction

Hold your upper lip in position (firm and full, smiling slightly) throughout the exercise.

Hold the contraction for five seconds.

Release.

Repeat the exercise until your muscles feel the burn.

Lip Press Muscle Diagram

These are the muscles you should feel when you are doing this exercise.

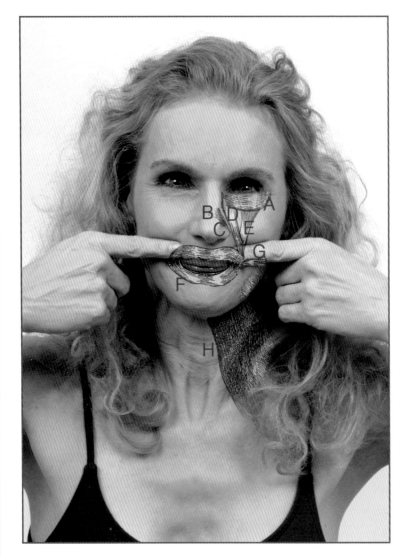

A. Orbicularis oculi

B. Dilator naris anterior

C. Dilator naris posterior

D. Levator labii superioris alaequa nasi

E. Levator labii superioris

F. Orbicularis oris

G. Risorius

H. Platysma myoides

CHEEK AREA
Cheek Enhancer

Level: **ADVANCED**

Area Worked: **CHEEKS**

Type of Exercise: **ISOTONIC**

The advanced Cheek Enhancer, like the beginning version, uses your fingertips to "hold" the muscles of your cheeks, resisting the forward movement of your mouth. The difference here is that you repeat the exercise continuously (you'll look something like a fish blowing bubbles), sliding your fingers farther up the cheek after each contraction to vary the location of the resistance.

Tip:

If you do not exercise daily, you will lose 6 percent of your muscle mass every ten years starting at the age of twenty. This is as true of your face as it is of your body. (Taken from Ted Broer, "Eat, Drink and Be Healthy" cassette series)

Assume the Correct Position

Facial Alignment

Flare your lips like a fish, making a long, slightly square shape with your mouth.

Extend your jaw forward.

Push up with your lower eyelids. Force your upper eyelids to stay open and keep your forehead smooth.

Flare your nostrils.

Facial Alignment

Inner Cheek Workout

Hand Alignment

Hold your hands in front of your face with your forearms vertical and your fingertips pointing toward the ceiling.

Place the middle and index fingers of each hand beside your nostrils.

Hand Alignment

Resistance

As you perform the following muscular contraction, firmly hold your cheek muscles with your fingertips.

Muscular Contraction

Push your lips forward by squeezing your cheeks together, narrowing the "O" of your mouth. Resist the forward motion of your cheek muscles with firm pressure from your fingertips as you elongate your mouth.

Hold the contraction for two seconds.

Muscular Contraction A

Muscular Contraction B

Release the contraction. But as you return to the open "O" position, slide your fingers a little bit farther up alongside your nose.

Repeat the muscular contraction, holding the muscle firmly, then sliding your fingers upward again as you release. Continue the sequence, ending when your fingers are just below your tear ducts.

Hold the final position for ten seconds.

Release.

Repeat the sequence until your muscles feel the burn.

Muscular Contraction C

Outer Cheek Workout

Hand Alignment

Hold your hands in front of your face with your forearms vertical and your fingertips pointing toward the ceiling.

Place your middle and ring fingers at the base of your cheeks, just above the corners of your lips.

Hand Alignment

Resistance

As you perform the following muscular contraction, firmly hold your cheek muscles with your fingertips.

Muscular Contraction

Push your lips forward by squeezing your cheeks together, narrowing the "O" of your mouth. Resist the forward motion of your cheek muscles with pressure from your fingertips as you elongate your mouth.

Hold each contraction for two seconds.

Muscular Contraction A

Muscular Contraction B

Release the contraction. But as you return to the open "O" position, slide your fingers a little bit further up your cheeks, fanning them slightly and moving them toward the outer corners of your eyes.

Repeat the muscular contraction, holding the muscle firmly, then sliding your fingers upward again as you release. Continue the sequence, ending when your fingers are fanned slightly along the top edge of your cheekbones, below the outer corners of your eyes.

Hold the final forward position of your mouth for ten seconds.

Release.

Repeat the sequence until your muscles feel the burn.

Muscular Contraction C

Cheek Enhancer Muscle Diagram

These are the muscles you should feel when you are doing this exercise.

A. Orbicularis oculi

B. Dilator naris anterior

C. Dilator naris posterior

D. Levator labii superioris alaequa nasi

E. Levator labii superioris

F. Zygomaticus minor

G. Zygomaticus major

H. Orbicularis oris

EYE AREA

Lid Up

Level: **ADVANCED**

Area Worked: **LOWER EYELIDS**

Type of Exercise: **ISOTONIC**

8

Now that you've learned to keep your forehead motionless during the beginning Lid Ups, you're going to use the tips of your fingers to add resistance. By building up the muscle that rings your eye (the orbicular oculis), you will literally open up the eye area, reducing the appearance of crow's-feet. As with all of the advanced exercises, you'll also be hardening the facial muscles for a full face workout.

8

Lid Up

Tip:

Eating too much salt can make your eyes puffy (and the rest of you, too). It also stresses your kidneys. (Taken from McKinley Health Center, University of Illinois, citing R. L. Duyff, *American Dietetic Association's Complete Food and Nutrition Guide*, 1998)

Caution:

Your fingertips are providing the resistance here, but the weight of your fingers gently resting on the muscle is enough. Be very careful not to press, poke, or pull. Your undereye area is as delicate as a butterfly's wing, so think of your fingertips as tiny barbells just heavy enough to give a butterfly a workout.

Caution:

Remove contact lenses before you begin this exercise and use extremely gentle pressure.

Fingernails long and sharp? Trim them, put on cotton gloves, or skip this exercise.

Assume the Correct Position

Facial Alignment

Tighten all the muscles of your face without wrinkling the skin.

Flatten your lips against your teeth, keeping them full and pressed together.

Slightly extend your jaw, while pressing upward with the corners of your lips. First your teeth should meet, then your lower teeth should extend slightly forward, still covered by your full, flat lips.

Extend your lower lip outward in a slight pout by pressing upward with your chin. Can you feel it in your neck?

Push upward with your lower eyelid muscles only. Keep your upper eyelids open and your forehead smooth.

Stretch your tongue toward the top of your mouth. Curl it back so that the bottom of your tongue touches the roof of your mouth, and keep pushing it back toward your throat.

Flare your nostrils.

Facial Alignment

Hand Alignment

Raise your elbows so that your forearms are parallel to the ground.

Place the tips of your first three fingers on the top edge of your cheekbones, just below the outer corners of your eyes.

Resistance

Use the tips of your first three fingers to resist the upward contraction of your lower eyelid muscles with a firm, light touch.

Muscular Contraction

Push up with your lower eyelids only. Your upper eyelids should stay open and your forehead should remain motionless. Don't squint. Flare your nostrils and keep your face taut.

Hold the contraction for two seconds.

Release.

Repeat the exercise until your muscles feel the burn.

Hand Alignment

Muscular Contraction

8

Lid Up

Lid Up Muscle Diagram

These are the muscles you should feel when you are doing this exercise.

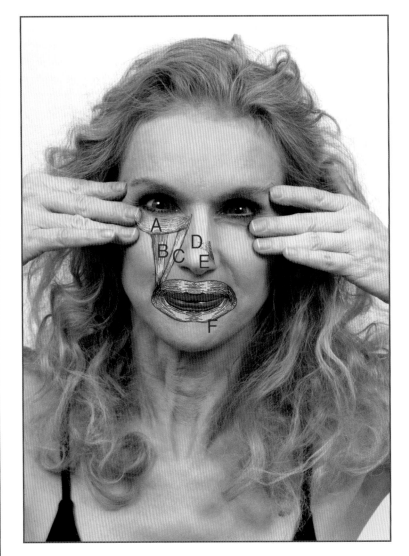

A. Orbicularis oculi

B. Levator labii superioris

C. Levator labii superioris alaequa nasi

D. Dilator naris anterior

E. Dilator naris posterior

F. Orbicularis oris

EYE AREA

Heavy Lids

Level: **ADVANCED**

Area Worked: **UPPER EYELIDS**

Type of Exercise: **ISOTONIC**

This is an exercise that benefits tremendously from the addition of the hard face. By bringing all the other muscles of the face into it, Heavy Lids becomes a rigorous exercise in precision control. Just don't get so caught up in the details that you forget to keep your brow smooth.

Tip:

The surgical lid lift (blepharoplasty) is the second most popular cosmetic facial procedure in America, right behind the nose job. According to the American Society of Plastic Surgeons, the average cost of this eyelid surgery is $2,544. If you live in California or New York, the cost can range up to $12,000.

Caution:

Remove contact lenses before you begin this exercise and use extremely gentle pressure.

Caution:

Fingernails long and sharp? Trim them, put on cotton gloves, or skip this exercise.

9

Heavy Lids

Assume the Correct Position

Facial Alignment

Tighten all the muscles of your face without wrinkling the skin.

Flatten your lips against your teeth, keeping them full and pressed together.

Slightly extend your jaw, while pressing upward with the corners of your lips. First your teeth should meet, then your lower teeth should extend slightly forward, still covered by your full, flat lips.

Extend your lower lip outward in a slight pout by pressing upward with your chin. Can you feel it in your neck?

Push upward with your lower eyelid muscles. Keep your upper eyelids open and your forehead smooth.

Stretch your tongue toward the top of your mouth. Curl it back so that the bottom of your tongue touches the roof of your mouth, and keep pushing it back toward your throat.

Flare your nostrils.

Close your eyes tightly.

Facial Alignment A

Facial Alignment B

Heavy Lids

9

Hand Alignment

Raise your elbows so that your forearms are parallel to the ground.

Gently rest the tips of your index fingers on the center of each upper eyelid.

Resistance

Resist the opening of your upper eyelids by holding with the firm but light touch of your index fingers.

Muscular Contraction

Try to force your eyes to open. Work the eyelids only. Do not lift with the eyebrow muscles.

Hold the contraction for two seconds.

Release.

Repeat the exercise until your muscles feel the burn.

Hand Alignment

Muscular Contraction

9

Heavy Lids

Heavy Lids Muscle Diagram

These are the muscles you should feel when you are doing this exercise.

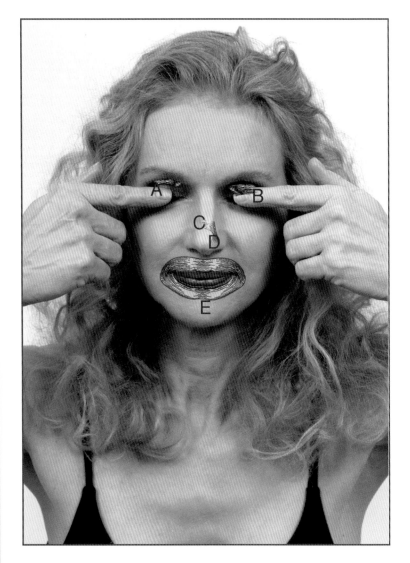

A. Levator palpebrae superioris

B. Orbicularis oculi pars palebral

C. Dilator naris anterior

D. Dilator naris posterior

E. Orbicularis oris

Brow Raiser

Level: **ADVANCED**

Area Worked: **EYEBROWS & FOREHEAD**

Type of Exercise: **ISOMETRIC**

The basic facial alignment for all three versions of the Brow Raiser is the same, though your hand placement will vary. We're making the exercise more difficult by hardening your facial alignment. When you achieve proficiency, this series of moves will quickly become your own personal tension-release ritual, something you do instead of reaching for the aspirin.

Tip:

The neurotoxin in Botox, when injected into the area around a vertical frown line, prevents the line from appearing by paralyzing the surrounding muscle. A strong muscle will not crease and furrow as readily as a weak one, and a little exercise can yield the same results as an expensive medical treatment.

Assume the Correct Position

Facial Alignment

Tighten all the muscles of your face without wrinkling the skin.

Flatten your lips against your teeth, keeping them full and pressed together.

Slightly extend your jaw, while pressing upward with the corners of your lips. First your teeth should meet, then your lower teeth should extend slightly forward, still covered by your full, flat lips.

Extend your lower lip outward in a slight pout by pressing upward with your chin. Can you feel it in your neck?

Push upward with your lower eyelid muscles. Keep your upper eyelids open and your forehead smooth.

Stretch your tongue toward the top of your mouth. Curl it back so that the bottom of your tongue touches the roof of your mouth, and keep pushing it back toward your throat.

Flare your nostrils.

Facial Alignment

Vertical Line Workout

Hand Alignment

Raise your elbows so that your forearms are parallel to the ground.

Place the first three fingers of each hand horizontally across your forehead just above your eyebrows with your fingertips meeting in the middle.

Resistance

Apply outward and upward pressure with your fingers to hold your forehead firmly in place.

Muscular Contraction

Attempt to scowl, trying to force your eyebrows inward and together against the pressure of your hands.

Hold the contraction for two seconds.

Release.

Repeat the exercise until your muscles feel the burn.

Hand Alignment

Muscular Contraction

10

Brow Raiser

Horizontal Line Workout

Hand Alignment

Hold your hands in front of your face.

Place the tips of the first three fingers of each hand above your eyebrows with your fingertips pointing upward.

Resistance

With downward pressure from your fingers, hold your forehead firmly in place.

Muscular Contraction

As if you are surprised, force your eyebrow muscles upward against the holding pressure of your hands.

Hold the contraction for two seconds.

Release.

Repeat the exercise until your muscles feel the burn.

Hand Alignment

Muscular Contraction

Eyebrow Workout

Hand Alignment

Raise your elbows so that your forearms are parallel to the ground.

Fan all of your fingertips out along your whole forehead, just above your eyebrows, with your fingertips pointing downward and your palms above your forehead.

Hand Alignment

Resistance

With upward pressure from your fingers, hold your forehead firmly in place.

Muscular Contraction

As if frowning, force your eyebrow muscles downward against the holding pressure of your hands.

Hold the contraction for two seconds.

Release.

Repeat the exercise until your muscles feel the burn.

Muscular Contraction

Brow Raiser Muscle Diagram

These are the muscles you should feel when you are doing this exercise.

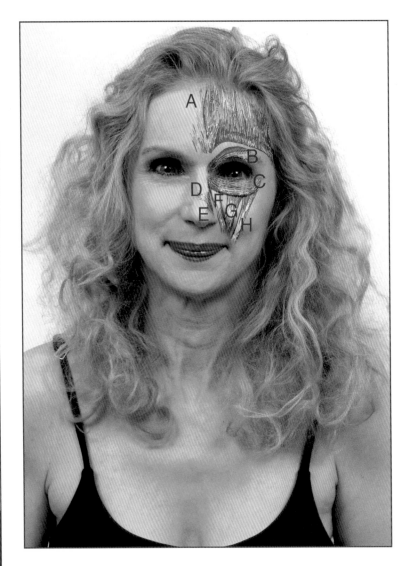

A. Occipitofrontalis (frontal portion)

B. Corrugator supercilii

C. Orbicularis oculi

D. Dilator naris anterior

E. Dilator naris posterior

F. Levator labii superioris alaequa nasi

G. Levator labii superioris

H. Zygomaticus minor

Hardface Insert with Muscle Overlay

This diagram illustrates the outward muscles of the face and neck. Ideally, after a good workout, you should feel like I look in the illustration; your muscles will be taut and sore if you have done the exercises correctly.

On the following page, you will find a list of the muscles illustrated in this diagram.

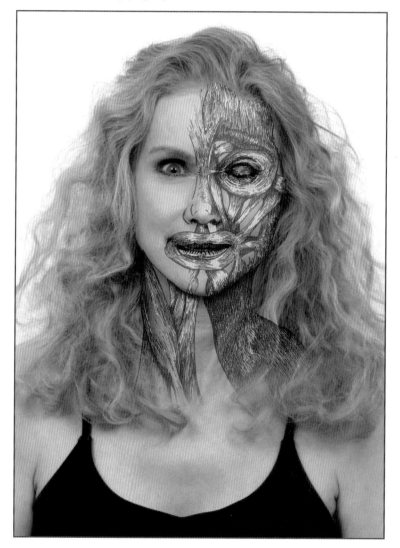

Legend

Occipitofrontalis
(partially cut away)
Insertion: skin of eyebrow,
root of nose

Procerus
Insertion: skin between
eyebrows

Corrugator supercilii
Insertion: skin of eyebrow

Orbiculoris oculi pars palebral
(orbital part)
Insertion: near origin after
encircling orbit

Orbiculoris oculi pars palebral
(palpebral part)
Insertion: orbital tubercle of
zygomatic bone

Levator labii superioris
alaeque nasi
Insertion: skin of upper lip,
ala of nose

Levator labii superioris
Insertion: upper lip and
margin of nostril

Auricularis anterior
Insertion: cartilage of ear

Dilator naris posterior
Insertion: side of nose
above nostril

Dilator naris anterior
Insertion: margin of nostril

Zygomaticus minor
Insertion: upper lip

Zygomaticus major
Insertion: angle of mouth

Levator anguli oris
Insertion: corner of mouth

Masseter
(partially cut away)
Insertion: ramus and angle
of lower jaw

Buccinator
Insertion: orbicular muscle
at angle of mouth

Risorius
Insertion: skin at angle of
mouth

Depressor septi nasi
Insertion: ala and septum of
nose

Orbicularis oris
Insertion: muscles interlace
to encircle mouth

Depressor anguli oris
Insertion: angle of mouth

Depressor labii inferioris
Insertion: lower lip

Mentalis
Insertion: skin of chin

Platysma myodies
Insertion: skin over
mandible and neck

Sternocleidomastoid
Insertion: mastoid process,
superior nuchal line of
occipital bone

Thyro-hyoid
Insertion: greater horn of
hyoid bone

Omo-hyoid
Insertion: lower border,
body of hyoid bone

Sterno-thyroid
Insertion: lower border of
body of hyoid bone

Cool Down Exercises

Cool Down Exercises

6

The cool down exercise massage allows your body to gradually relax and restores muscle integrity through stretching and massaging. The following invigorating massage technique is an excellent way to complete your workout. It can also be beneficial as a quick pick-me-up for your face when you don't have enough time for all of the exercises. You can even perform the cool down exercise massage while washing and applying skin care products to your face and neck. Pay attention to the direction in which you make the strokes—this is the way you should apply moisturizer or night cream. For a particularly luxurious massage experience, apply your night cream while you do these exercises. You will encourage circulation, which, in turn, will stimulate and tone your face and promote healthy skin and muscles.

Tip:

Stress and tension stimulate the body's oil-producing sebaceous glands, which increases the incidence of breakouts and pimples. (Taken from www.syence.com)

Cool Down Exercise Arrow Diagram

This diagram illustrates the correct direction as well as the suggested sequence in which to stroke the muscles.

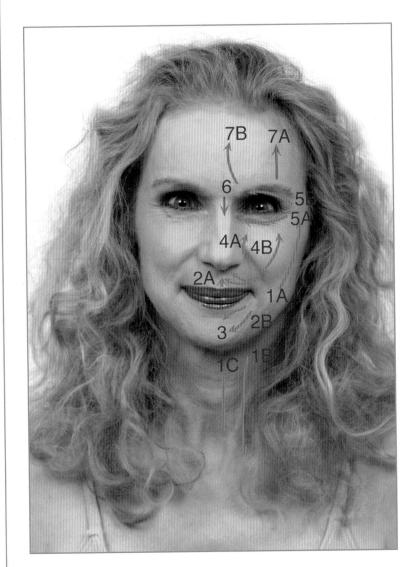

1A. Jaw: Stroke upward

1B. Neck: Stroke downward

1C. Neck: Stroke downward

2A. Mouth: Roll upward

2B. Mouth: Roll downward

3. Chin: Stroke downward

4. Cheeks: Slide upward

5. Eyes: Pat gently

6. Eyebrows: Stroke downward

7. Forehead: Stroke upward

Assume the Correct Position

Facial Alignment

Tighten all the muscles of your face without wrinkling the skin.

Flatten your lips against your teeth, keeping them full and pressed together.

Slightly extend your jaw, while pressing upward with the corners of your lips. First your teeth should meet, then your lower teeth should extend slightly forward, still covered by your full, flat lips.

Extend your lower lip outward in a slight pout by pressing upward with your chin. Can you feel it in your neck?

Push upward with your lower eyelid muscles. Keep your upper eyelids open and your forehead smooth.

Stretch your tongue toward the top of your mouth. Curl it back so that the bottom of your tongue touches the roof of your mouth, and keep pushing it back toward your throat.

Flare your nostrils.

Facial Alignment

Hand Alignment

In this series of exercise massages, you will use your hands to make smooth, alternating strokes.

Jaw/Neck Exercise

Turn your head slightly to the right. Move your mouth right, stretching the left side of your face flat. Remember to keep tension in all your muscles.

Starting with your left side, use an upward stroke from the hinge of your jawbone toward your cheekbone, alternating hands as you move up your face.

Jaw/Neck A

Beginning under the left ear, behind the jawbone, make long downward strokes with alternating hands, ending at your collarbone.

As you continue stroking, work your hands around from under your ear all the way to the center of your neck (where your Adam's apple is).

Jaw/Neck B

Jaw/Neck C

As you reach the center, turn your head to the left and move your mouth to the left, flattening the right side of your face.

Continue stroking until you reach the area under your right ear.

Repeat for the right side of your face.

Repeat the entire sequence three times.

Jaw/Neck D

Jaw/Neck E

Mouth Exercise

Place the sides of your index fingers horizontally along the upper edge of your lips, centered above the corners of your mouth with your fingertips pointing at each other.

Roll your fingers to produce an upward pull on your lip. Your fingernails will rotate away from your skin, turning toward the mirror. Continue to keep your mouth hard and flat, resisting the upward pull.

Repeat the roll, moving your fingers inward with each stroke, until your fingertips meet above the center of your lips.

Mouth A

Mouth B

Next, place the sides of your index fingers horizontally along the lower edge of your lips, centered below the corners of your mouth with your fingertips pointing at each other.

Roll your fingers to produce a downward pull on your lip. Your fingernails will rotate in toward your mouth. Continue to keep your mouth hard and flat, resisting the downward pull.

Repeat the roll, moving your fingers inward with each stroke, until your fingertips meet.

Repeat the entire sequence three times.

Mouth C

Mouth D

Chin Exercise

Lay the sides of your index fingers, flat and horizontal, below the corners of your mouth.

Stroke firmly downward to your jawbone, following the curve of your chin; think of drawing a set of parentheses.

Repeat the movement, moving inward toward your chin. End by drawing a circle around the ball of your chin with your fingers. Do not do this movement on the center mound of your chin.

Chin A

Chin B

Cheek Exercise

Open your mouth into a long "O" shape. Keep it open throughout the cheek exercise.

Place your middle fingers next to each nostril with your fingertips pointing upward.

Applying firm pressure, slowly slide your fingers along the sides of your nose, until they are just inside the corners of your eyes.

Inner Cheek A

Inner Cheek B

Next, place your ring, middle, and index fingers next to each corner of your mouth.

Slide your fingers upward and outward, fanning them toward the apices of your cheeks and ending the stroke with fingers slightly spread along the top edges of your cheekbones, below the outer corners of your eyes.

Repeat the sequence three times.

Outer Cheek A

Outer Cheek B

Eye Area Exercise

Place the tips of your two middle fingers at the outer corners of your eyes.

Gently pat along the bony ridges of your eye sockets, under your eyes, working toward the inner corners.

Outer Eye

Under Eye

Repeat, patting along the upper ridges of your eye sockets, again moving inward.

Repeat the sequence three times.

Upper Eye A

Upper Eye B

Eyebrow Exercise

Position your index fingers at the bridge of your nose, between your eyebrows.

Make short downward strokes, reaching halfway down your nose, alternating fingers.

Repeat the motion on each side of your nose, under your inner eyebrow.

Repeat this sequence three times.

Eyebrow A

Eyebrow B

Forehead Exercise

Begin at the left side of your forehead, above your eyebrow, and stroke upward toward your hairline.

Use the entire flat side of your two middle fingers to make long, upward strokes.

Alternating your hands, move across your forehead to the right side.

Repeat the sequence three times.

Forehead A

Forehead B

Lifestyle

CHAPTER

Lifestyle

7

How you wash your face can make a difference in how you age. This is because the skin and the underlying muscles can be subject to stretching over time if you continually pull and scrub them in a direction contrary to their nature. In Chapter 1 of this book, we discussed the concept of origin and insertion as it relates to muscle tissue, and it bears repeating here. Every muscle in your body has a point of origin, where it attaches to bone, and a point of insertion, where it attaches to a moving part, either bone or soft tissue. When you massage a muscle, you must always stroke from insertion to origin and never the other way around. Stroking the muscle in the wrong direction will cause it to stretch over time and become loose and saggy. Because the skin and muscles of the face are delicate, they are particularly susceptible to abuse. Exfoliate no more than once a week, and even then, do so gently. A gentle exfoliation using circular strokes can make your skin glow, but if you're making your circles in the wrong direction, you will be hastening the aging process.

Tip:

Bags and wrinkles can be exacerbated by all that tugging and scrubbing you inflict on your delicate lower eyelids while taking off your mascara at the end of the day. To avoid this, get in the habit of doing a Lid Up while you remove your makeup, tensing the lower eyelid. This will prevent the skin from being stretched as you gently daub it with a washrag or cotton ball. And remember to always stroke inward—patting from the outer corner of your eye toward the bridge of your nose.

Lifestyle Arrow Diagram

This diagram illustrates the correct direction as well as the suggested sequence in which to wash and dry your face.

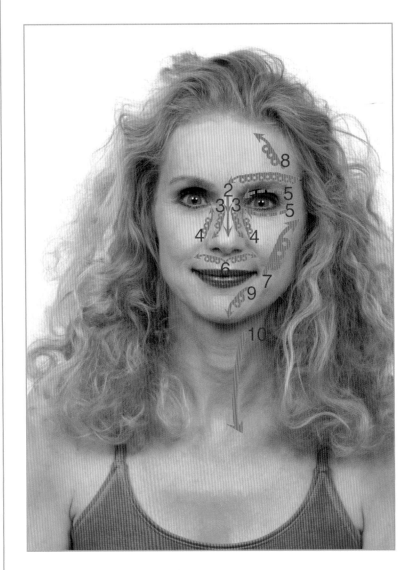

1. Stroke inward
   (circular motion)

2. Stroke downward

3. Stroke downward
   (circular motion)

4. Stroke upward
   (circular motion)

5. Pat gently

6. Stroke outward
   (circular motion)

7. Stroke upward
   (circular motion)

8. Stroke upward
   (circular motion)

9. Stroke downward
   (circular motion)

How to Wash Your Face

Whether using a soft washcloth or just your fingers, wash your face as follows:

Starting at the temples, work inward along your eyebrows using short, circular strokes. Moving downward, make short strokes from the bridge to the tip of your nose and small circular strokes along the sides of your nose.

Make small circular upward strokes moving from the base of the flare of your nostrils toward the inner corners of your eyes.

On your upper and lower lids, pat gently from the outer corners of your eyes inward—do not scrub or wipe in this area. Women are particularly rough on the eye area while washing, since they are often removing makeup. A good eye-makeup remover that takes the mascara off without rubbing is a must if you wear waterproof mascara. If you are wiping your eyes with a tissue, always keep the eye tissue firm, either by tensing your lower lids or by holding it in place with your fingers.

On your upper lip, beginning from the center, make small circular strokes, moving upward and outward toward your cheeks.

Make upward sweeping, circular strokes on your cheeks and then your forehead.

Make small downward circular strokes on your chin finishing with sweeping downward strokes on your neck.

Be sure to use these same movements while drying your face.

Tip:

Salt is an acquired taste. This means that, while the foods you eat will taste bland when you first cut back on salt, soon your taste buds will adapt and you won't even notice the difference. In fact, the foods you eat will probably taste better than ever when you stop dulling your senses with so much salt. You can look better and add years to your life by cutting back on salt. (Taken from McKinley Health Center, University of Illinois, citing R. L. Duyff, *American Dietetic Association's Complete Food and Nutrition Guide*, 1998)

A Word on Diet: Nine Do's and a Don't

Why talk about diet in a book about facial exercise? Many patients in my practice as a paramedical aesthetician have been told by their family doctors that diet has no impact on the skin's health and that supplements just give one expensive urine. Yet in every case I have treated, when eating habits were changed and proper supplementation was given, skin problems cleared up. The patients also experienced some wonderful side effects, such as better digestion, an increase in energy, and weight loss. This all resulted from treating a skin problem.

What follows is a set of dietary rules. Follow them the way you follow the exercise regimen: at your own pace and as they fit into your lifestyle. Remember, even if you only adopt one new dietary habit—substituting whole-grain breads for refined flours, for example, or eliminating hydrogenated oils from your diet—you'll be improving your appearance. That these tidbits of advice also pertain to longevity, cancer prevention, and a healthy heart is merely a happy coincidence.

RULE No. 1. Drink water!

Two-thirds of your body is composed of water, and you lose about ten glasses throughout the day (five and one-half glasses via urination, one-half glass via the bowels, two glasses through exhaling, and two glasses from perspiration). Side effects from dehydration include kidney infections and stones, mild depression, mental sluggishness, body odor, halitosis, and strong-smelling urine. Divide your body weight by two to get the number of ounces of water your body requires daily. If you exercise or drink coffee and/or alcohol, drink even more water. Always drink distilled or highly filtered water.

RULE No. 2. Eat butter and olive oil.

Many people hate margarine. And guess what? It's bad for you. Margarine is a hydrogenated oil, also known as a trans-fatty acid. Hydrogenation is a process used to thicken oils to create products like margarine or Crisco, and since hydrogenation increases shelf life, it's widely used in most packaged foods. Unfortunately, the process also releases free radicals, which cause cancer. If you're going to make just one dietary change, eliminating these oils is a good choice. They lurk in every corner of the supermarket—in margarine, candy bars, most baked goods, and prepared foods like chips. You need to read labels assiduously to avoid them. Any oil can be rendered unhealthy through the hydrogenation process—even healthy ones like olive or canola oil. Even that tofu cream cheese you serve so proudly is full of hydrogenated oils.

The good news is that you're far better off eating butter in moderation. An even better alternative is to mix cold pressed olive oil, herbs, and butter to create a delicious spread.

RULE No. 3. Eat meat!

Protein fortifies the body's tissues and organs because it provides all the necessary amino acids (building blocks for the body). Protein comes in two groups: complete proteins, found in dairy foods, fish, meat, and poultry, and incomplete proteins, found in grains, legumes, and leafy green vegetables. Incomplete proteins need to be combined with each other to give you adequate amounts of aminos. Eat three to five ounces of protein for two of your three daily meals. For a more accurate count, divide your body weight by fifteen and try to eat that many ounces daily.

Proteins are probably the tastiest of foods. Try fresh fish and young poultry, lamb, and veal (all must be organically fed, hormone, steroid, and antibiotic free). Avoid shellfish, farmed fish, and pork altogether. Eat meat rare, rather than well done—except for poultry, which must be thoroughly cooked. As a general rule, do not heat fresh foods over 110 degrees Fahrenheit. It will damage the enzymes and nutrients in them.

If you're a vegetarian, you need to take a complete blend of amino acids (see rule No. 8) in order to complete your protein requirements.

RULE No. 4. Eat it raw!

You will never gain weight by eating large quantities of raw or lightly steamed vegetables. Try chopping seven to ten different vegetables, mixing them together, and eating them twice a day. Adding sprouts, beans, legumes, nuts, and seeds boosts the nutrient value and the taste. Remember not to overcook vegetables. If you heat your food above 110 degrees Fahrenheit, you will destroy the enzymes and nutrients. Raw is perfect, but steaming or grilling will do.

RULE No. 5. Eat whole fruits!

Fruits are one of the richest sources of simple carbohydrates for your body. Yet even these types of sugars need to be eaten in moderation—no more than two or three small pieces of fruit per day, or the equivalent in a fruit salad. Sprinkle the fruit with rice fiber or bran to help slow the body's absorption. This helps keep blood sugar as balanced as possible.

You may be surprised to learn that fruit juices should be avoided. Juicing removes all the fiber from the fruit, leaving only simple sugars.

RULE No. 6. Get plenty of dietary fiber.

Fiber is a valuable form of carbohydrates and is essential to a healthy colon. It retains water, causing softer and heavier stools. This prevents constipation and lowers the risk of colon cancer. It also binds fats and substances that would result in the forming of cholesterol and carries them out of the body. If you ingest fiber products in addition to your regular whole grain, vegetable, and fruit intake, you also need to drink more water or the fiber will have the opposite of its intended effect and produce constipation.

RULE No. 7. Eat whole grains.

Some people crave breads and cannot live without them. Multi-whole grain sprouted breads are a good choice; they are some of the tastiest breads available.

Refined flours have no nutritional value; in fact, they clog the intestines, causing poor absorption of nutrients and forming a gluelike substance throughout the digestive tract. What grain-based products contain refined flours? Read the label. Look for four to five grams of fiber per serving, a good indication that whole grains have been used. Organic products are almost always unrefined. Also keep an eye out for nontraditional grains, which can be excellent substitutes. This means grains like brown rice, basmati rice, amaranth, millet, buckwheat, groats, and quinoa. The variety available is huge, so you are bound to find some that you like. Avoid the more common—and less healthy—grains like wheat, barley, and oats. These familiar grains have been genetically engineered to contain less protein and five times the gluten, which is highly allergenic and difficult for our bodies to process. Stay away from them.

RULE No. 8. Take your vitamins.

Since American soil has become deficient in a full range of nutrients, the food we get from it is also deficient in nutrients. For starters, choose a daily multivitamin with a full range of antioxidants, vitamins, minerals, and phytonutrients. Look for "bioavailable" forms of these vitamins, which come in forms that are readily absorbed by the body, and always buy them in liquid, powder, or capsule form instead of hard tablets, which are difficult to absorb.

Free radicals accelerate the aging process. These unstable atoms have at least one unpaired electron, making it easy for them to attach themselves to healthy atoms in our bodies and destroy them. Antioxidants neutralize harmful free radicals. The antioxidants include the vitamins A, C, and E, the mineral zinc, alpha-lipoic acid, grape seed extract, and polyphenol, the pure concentrate of green tea. The king of antioxidants is stabilized rice bran, a soluble, whole food nutrient that contains over seventy-four different antioxidants and tastes wonderful sprinkled over yogurt or mixed in a shake.

Amino acids help your skin to hold more moisture, stay softer, and retain firmness and elasticity. They also help burn excess fat and aid digestion. Amino acids are the building blocks that make up proteins. Chicken eggs are one of the most complete forms of protein found in nature, but all animal proteins are excellent sources of amino acids. When shopping for supplements, look for "free-form" amino acids (molecules that have been extracted from the protein chain of foods) and look for a full spectrum of at least eighteen to twenty-two listed aminos in a "complete blend." Complete blends mimic the proportions found in natural eggs or meats. Also choose the "L" form of the amino acid (L-Lysine, L-Arginine, and so on) because these amino acids will be readily absorbed, rather than going through a major digestive process as protein powders must do.

Essential fatty acids (EFAs) are a must for beautiful skin, hair, and nails and assist in reducing the recovery time of fatigued muscles after exercise. They also aid in the prevention of heart disease, arthritis, candida albicans (intestinal yeast overgrowth), psoriasis, and memory degeneration. Fatty acids transport minerals and nutrients into the body and carry toxins out. The main ones you'll find available in supplement form include flaxseed oil, evening primrose oil, borage oil, grape seed oil, and fish oil. Rubbing borage oil on eczema can work wonders.

Probiotics help correct or prevent numerous skin conditions such as acne, psoriasis, and eczema. They also help with bowel and urinary tract problems. How do they work? Our digestive tract is naturally inhabited by good bacteria that help it clean itself out. But stress and our heavy use of antibiotics and pesticides kill them. Probiotic supplements such as lactobacillus acidophilus and bifidobacterium bifidum help to restore the balance of good bacteria in our digestive tract for a clean and healthy colon and beautiful skin.

RULE No. 9. Exercise.

Exercise improves physical appearance by strengthening the body and by increasing blood circulation to the skin. It also increases life span, boosts energy, and raises the body's defense against cancer, diabetes, and osteoporosis, while decreasing mental anxiety, depression, blood pressure, cholesterol levels, and the risk of heart disease.

Your exercise routine should include daily stretching, twenty to thirty minutes of cardiovascular activity three to five times weekly, and fifteen to twenty minutes of weight training three times a week.

RULE No. 10. Avoid substances that are bad for you.

You know what you shouldn't consume, but let's round up the usual suspects anyway: caffeine, artificial sweeteners, monosodium glutamate, alcohol, junk food, tobacco, chlorinated/fluoridated water, and salt.

Vigilance is required, as these substances lurk in most processed foods. For example, if you think that a can of diet soda is harmless, think again. Soft drinks deplete the body of calcium and also contain aluminum by-products, which have been linked to Alzheimer's disease.

Other products that contain aluminum include baking powder/baking soda, antacids, salt, cookware, and deodorants. Read labels and buy the brands that don't contain it. Also avoid aluminum cookware and always use wax paper between aluminum foil and food.

The problems with diet soda don't stop there: artificial sweeteners like aspartame and saccharine are carcinogenic. And caffeine raises LDL (bad) cholesterol levels and stresses the adrenal glands, which leads to out-of-control blood sugar levels.

Instead, how about a nice tall glass of antioxidant-rich iced green tea? You can use the herbal sweetener, Stevia, or my favorite, a new no-calorie sweetener with no aftertaste, derived from sprouted mung bean extract. It's marketed by Suzanne Somers (she of Thighmaster fame) under the brand name SomerSweet and is available so far only through the Internet.

In conclusion, know that your diet affects your face both directly and indirectly. If you take in plenty of vitamins and nutrients, your skin will have everything it needs on a cellular level to take care of itself with a minimum of fuss on your part—staying healthy can be a great time-saver, if you choose to look at it that way. As for the indirect benefits of making dietary changes, remember that a healthy body is better able to contend with the stresses of daily life. If you're wired on caffeine or weighed down by sugar, you will be much more likely to experience stress, and as a result you are far more likely to engage in facial habits like frowning and scowling. So take your vitamins, eat your vegetables, and smile.

Making It Work

With this book in hand, you have some powerful tools at your disposal for changing the way you look and the way you feel. But having the tools and using them are very different. Almost everyone has had the experience of beginning a program of self-improvement only to set it aside when life gets too busy or stressful. More often than not, the program is never picked up again, and all you've gained for your well-intentioned efforts is a sense of guilt and failure. In this way, self-improvement sometimes does more harm than good.

The Eigard Method is designed for maximum flexibility. The skills in this book, once learned, are forever at your disposal. If all you get from reading it is a new perspective on how your face ages, then the time will have been well spent. If you also learn the correct way to take off your makeup in the evening, then the experience becomes an investment in your future. If you use the method to avoid a face-lift and spend the difference between the cost of this book and major surgery on a trip to Paris or a new wardrobe, then good for you. But remember that the fact that you picked up the book at all is grounds for self-congratulation.

To help you envision the ways in which the various components of The Eigard Method can be integrated into daily life, let's look at a day in the life of a typical student of the method.

7:30 A.M.

Time to wake up. Instead of hitting the snooze button, you hang your head over the edge of the bed and give yourself a ten-minute Warm Up exercise massage. Before rising, you perform exercise No. 1, the Neck Lift.

8:00 A.M.

After washing your face with small circular motions that mimic the Warm Up exercise massage, you are ready to perform a couple of exercises. Since you have always wanted to have cheeks like Katharine Hepburn's, you choose to focus on your cheeks. You perform exercise No. 7 if you're running late or have a morning meeting to prepare for. If not, you also do No. 5.

9:00 A.M.

Instead of coffee, a cup of antioxidant-rich green tea jump-starts your day.

10:00 A.M.

Seated at the cubicle in your office, you get ready to return several phone calls that came while you were in an early meeting. You have hung a small mirror on the wall, next to the picture of your family, and you watch your facial expressions while you talk, taking note of the way your lip curls to the side when you tell a joke.

3:30 P.M.

Working to meet a 5:00 P.M. project deadline, you find yourself developing a tension headache. You pause, and instead of taking a walk to the water cooler, you straighten your chair in front of your mirror and perform three sets of exercise No. 10 to relieve the tension in your forehead, forestall the headache, and restore a sense of calm.

6:30 P.M.

Time for a brief chat with your best friend. You've hung a mirror in the telephone alcove, and while you talk, you notice your facial expressions. You tell her the same joke you told at work, and this time you don't make the sideways motion with your mouth, keeping a slight smile on your face instead.

7:30 P.M.

Dinner is a salad of chopped vegetables and hormone-free, organic lamb chops, cooked rare. Since there's very little preparation or cooking time involved in this meal, most of your evening is free for reading or watching a movie.

10:00 P.M.

Your nightly face-washing ritual incorporates the moves you learned in the Warm Up exercise massage. With a clean face, you sit down at your dresser and perform exercises No. 2 and No. 3. You perform the Cool Down exercise massage as you apply your night cream. The day's tension melts away.

Some days you will do more than others, to be sure, but isn't that true in everything you do? The lesson to be learned is that good habits and bad habits are in some ways no different: If you have time in your life for bad habits, or even if you once did, then you have time to practice The Eigard Method. If you have time to eat a pint of ice cream, you have time to practice The Eigard Method. If you have time to scowl, you have time to smile. What's required of you isn't a time commitment, but a change of attitude.

A Word in Closing

Your face is a map, giving observant fellow travelers directions to your very soul. Every experience you have ever lived through, for better or for worse, is etched on your face. If you take the time to love your life, and love yourself, and to train your face with as much care and discipline as you train the muscles of your body, the results will show. You will stop trying to look the way you looked at thirty, or twenty. Why erase a life when you can improve upon it in your looks and in your heart? When you are truly fit and ready to face the future, you will find that your face, like your heart, has a far more elegant and beautiful profile at forty, or sixty, than it ever had before.

Beauty is God's handwriting—a
wayside sacrament. Welcome it in
every fair face, in every fair sky,
in every flower, and thank God for it
as a cup of blessing.

—*Ralph Waldo Emerson*

Glossary

Auricularis anterior – The muscle located just in front of the ear; it draws the ear forward and upward.

Body alignment – The proper positioning of the body muscles for performing an exercise.

Buccinator – The muscle at the sides of the mouth responsible for drawing the lips back in a smile (also causes the cheeks to contract). This is the muscle you use when blowing out candles.

Burn – In exercise, working the muscle to the point of extreme weakness or fatigue, where a burning sensation is felt.

Continuously – In exercise, an action performed without break, pause, or interruption.

Contraction – The drawing back or tensing of a muscle (see "muscular contraction").

Cool Down – An activity that lowers the intensity of exercise and returns the body back to normal blood flow and its original, pre-exercise state.

Corrugator supercilii – The muscle responsible for frown lines. Located in the eyebrow area, this muscle controls frowning as eyebrows come together by being drawn downward and inward.

Depressor anguli oris – The muscles running from the corners of the mouth to the lower jaw (chin).

Depressor labii inferioris – The muscles running from the lower lip to the center of the chin.

Depressor septi nasi – The short muscle that lies between the mucous membrane and the muscular structure of the lip; it constricts the nostrils.

Dilator naris anterior – The muscles running from the top of the nose to the sides of the nose, over cartilage, responsible for flaring the nostrils (see also "dilator naris posterior").

Dilator naris posterior – The muscles at the sides of the nose, responsible for flaring the nostrils (see also "dilator naris anterior").

Firm pressure – Steady, strong application of pressure.

Flexibility – The ability of a joint to move through a normal range of motion. An increase in a joint's flexibility can improve exercise performance and lower the risk of injury. This is achieved by stretching.

Hand alignment – The proper positioning of the hands (muscles and finger position) for performing an exercise.

Infra-hyoid region – These muscles lower the larynx and hyoid bone, after they have been raised during swallowing; they are also concerned with the drawing in of air.

> Sterno-hyoid
> Sterno-thyroid
> Thyro-hyoid
> Omo-hyoid

Insertion – In exercise physiology, the point where a muscle attaches to a moving part, either bone or tissue. The opposite of the point of origin.

Isometric contraction – A muscular contraction in which the muscle tenses in both directions, without shortening or lengthening, causing no movement in the joint.

Isotonic contraction – A muscular contraction in which the muscle tenses in a single direction at a time, shortening or lengthening to allow movement of the joint.

Lateral pterygoid – The muscles on the sides of the face that, along with the masseters, move the lower jaw up and down, opening and closing the mouth.

Levator anguli oris – This muscle raises the angle of the mouth.

Levator labii superioris – The muscles that run from the middle of the inner cheek to the upper lip, helping to move the upper lip, along with the levator labii superioris alaque nasi.

Levator labii superioris alaeque nasi – the muscles along the sides of the nose that work to lift the upper lip, along with the levator labii superioris.

Levator palpebrae superioris – The upper eyelid muscle; lifts and lowers the upper eyelid.

Light pressure – In exercise, a gentle touch that holds a muscle in place but does not compress the tissues beneath.

Masseter – The muscles running from the outer corner of the jawbone to the outer cheekbones, responsible, along with the lateral pterygoid and the medial pterygoid, for opening and closing the mouth.

Medial pterygoid – The muscles running from the middle cheekbone to the lower jaw, responsible, along with the lateral pterygoid and the masseter, for opening and closing the mouth.

Mentalis – This is the muscle that raises the fleshy part of the chin.

Muscular alignment – The arrangement of muscles to create proper posture.

Muscular contraction – Produced when a skeletal muscle, or group of muscles, is stimulated. Muscular contractions may be isometric or isotonic.

Occipitofrontalis – The wide, flat, vertical muscle that spans the forehead and raises and lowers the eyebrows.

Orbicularis oculi pars palebral – The circular muscle that rings the eye, responsible for winking and squinting.

Orbicularis oris – The circular muscle that rings the mouth, responsible for opening and closing the lips.

Origin – In exercise physiology, the point where a muscle attaches to (nonmoving) bone. The opposite of the point of insertion.

Palatoglossus – The muscle that lifts the tongue.

Platysma myodies – The muscle that runs from the jawline to the front of the neck, tightening the skin on the neck.

Pout – The act of pushing the lower lip out to appear swollen.

Procerus – The thin sheath of muscle between the eyes over the nasal bone; the muscle draws the eyebrows together and down, wrinkling the bridge of the nose.

Risorius – The muscle that pulls the corners of the mouth straight back.

Scalenus anterior – The muscles at the side of the neck that, when contracted, bend the neck to one side or the other.

Skeletal muscles – Muscles attached to the bones via tendons. When contracted, skeletal muscles may allow movement of the skeletal system to occur.

Sternocleidomastoid – The muscles that run from the sides to the front of the neck, responsible for extending or rotating the head.

Styloglossus – The muscle that lifts and pulls back the tongue.

Supra-hyoid region – The muscles under the jaw that assist in swallowing.

> Digastric
> Stylo-hyoid
> Mylo-hyoid
> Genio-hyoid

Tendons – Soft tissue connectors that anchor skeletal muscles to bones. Muscles typically are attached to the bones by at least two tendons: one at the point of insertion and another at the point of origin.

Trapezius – The muscle at the back of the neck that moves the scapula (shoulder blade). Its lower portion extends down the back.

Warm Up – An activity that increases the blood flow to the skeletal muscles and elevates body temperature, preparing the body for exercise and reducing the possibility of injury.

Zygomaticus major – The muscle in the outer cheek area that lifts the mouth to smile and laugh with an upward and backward pull.

Zygomaticus minor – The muscle in the cheek area that draws the mouth into a sad (frowning) expression.

Index

TOLA PUBLISHING

Order Form

THE
EIGARD
METHOD

> You can have a lifetime of facial fitness—
> without surgery!

Please send the following products:

Quantity	Price	Item Description	Total
	$24.95	*The Eigard Method: Lifetime Facial Fitness without Plastic Surgery* Book	

Name:

Address:

City: State: Zip:

Tel #:   E-mail:

Payment Information:

☐ Check   Credit Card: ☐ Visa   ☐ MC   ☐ Amex

Card Number:

Name on Card: Exp. Date:

Signature

Ordering Information

Sales Tax:
Please add 8.25% sales tax to all orders shipped to California.
Shipping & Handling:
Books: UPS Ground $8.05 for 1st book; $1.00 for each additional
                      (allow 7–10 business days for delivery)
         3-day $12.30 for 1st book; $2.00 for each additional
         2-day $14.53 for 1st book; $3.00 for each additional
         Overnight $33.56 for 1st book; $5.00 for each additional
         US mailpriority $3.85
         Express $17.85

Fax Orders:
1.818.881.6789
Telephone Orders:
1.877.200.7878
Please have your credit card ready
Online Orders:
www.theeigardmethod.com
Mail Orders:
9663 Santa Monica Boulevard, #814
Beverly Hills, California 90210-4303 U.S.A.